COOPERATION OR CONFLICT
IN THE TAIWAN STRAIT?

COOPERATION OR CONFLICT IN THE TAIWAN STRAIT?

Ralph N. Clough

ROWMAN & LITTLEFIELD PUBLISHERS, INC.
Lanham • Boulder • New York • Oxford

H-Y LIB
(W)

HARVARD-YENCHING LIBRARY
HARVARD UNIVERSITY
2 DIVINITY AVENUE
CAMBRIDGE, MA 02138

YANKEE
03/09/1999

DS
799.847
.C59
1998

ROWMAN & LITTLEFIELD PUBLISHERS, INC.

Published in the United States of America
by Rowman & Littlefield Publishers, Inc.
4720 Boston Way, Lanham, Maryland 20706

12 Hid's Copse Road
Cumnor Hill, Oxford OX2 9JJ, England

Copyright © 1999 by Rowman & Littlefield Publishers, Inc.

All rights reserved. No part of this publication may be reproduced,
stored in a retrieval system, or transmitted in any form or by any
means, electronic, mechanical, photocopying, recording, or otherwise,
without the prior permission of the publisher.

British Library Cataloguing in Publication Information Available

Library of Congress Cataloging-in-Publication Data

Clough, Ralph N., 1916-
    Cooperation or conflict in the Taiwan strait? / Ralph N. Clough.
        p.   cm.
    Includes bibliographical references and index.
    ISBN 0-8476-9325-2 (alk. paper). — ISBN 0-8476-9326-0 (pbk. :
alk. paper)
        1. Taiwan — Politics and government — 1988- 2. China — Politics and
    government — 1976- 3. Chinese reunification question; 1949 —
    4. Taiwan — Relations — China. 5. China — Relations — Taiwan.
    I. Title.
    DS799.847.C59   1999
    327.5105124'9'09049 — dc21   98-39356
                                                                CIP

Printed in the United States of America

∞ ™ The paper used in this publication meets the minimum requirements of
American National Standard for Information Sciences—Permanence of Paper
for Printed Library Materials, ANSI Z39.48–1984.

To Awana

Contents

Preface

In March 1996, in an effort to intimidate the government and people of Taiwan, the People's Republic of China (PRC) fired two short-range ballistic missiles into splash zones within fifty miles of Kaohsiung, Taiwan's principal port, and two more within thirty miles of its second port, Keelung. It also conducted live-fire ground, air, and naval exercises along the coast of Fujian opposite Taiwan. The United States, in support of its long-held position that force must not be used to determine the future of Taiwan, deployed two carrier battle groups to the vicinity of Taiwan. This confrontation was the first between the military forces of the United States and the PRC since the offshore island crisis of the late 1950s. It drew to the attention of the American people the dangerous possibility that the differing policies of the governments in Washington and Beijing on the Taiwan issue could lead to military conflict.

The relationship between Taiwan and mainland China is dominated by two broad trends, one that draws them together and another that holds them apart. Ever since the government of the Republic of China (ROC) on Taiwan authorized travel to the mainland in 1987, trade, travel, investments, and other forms of cross-strait interchange have grown rapidly, creating an expanding network of people-to-people links and drawing together these two Chinese-speaking societies. On the other hand, the ROC has resisted political linkage to the mainland in the form of PRC proposals to make Taiwan a special administrative region of the PRC, similar to Hong Kong but with a higher degree of autonomy.

The two governments have battled each other fiercely in the international arena, with the PRC insisting on the exclusive right to represent China, including Taiwan, in the world community and the ROC maintaining, as a sovereign political entity, that has never been a part of or been controlled by the PRC, it has the right to its own diplomatic and official relations with other countries. A trip made by President Lee

Teng-hui to the United States, in an effort to enhance the ROC's international image, triggered the PRC's military reaction—a serious warning to the United States and Taiwan that it would not tolerate an independent state of Taiwan.

Political trends within Taiwan have accentuated the differences between Beijing and Taipei over Taiwan's status. During the past ten years, Taiwan has evolved from authoritarian rule to a fully democratic system, with a popularly elected president and legislature. The Kuomintang (KMT), which governed China on the mainland and has governed Taiwan since its withdrawal from the mainland in 1949, finds its position as ruling party threatened by the rise of a popular opposition, the Democratic Progressive Party (DPP). The KMT advocates the reunification of Taiwan with mainland China in the presumably distant future when the political system there has become democratic, but the DPP wants an independent Republic of Taiwan, which the PRC is determined to prevent, by the use of military force if necessary.

Whether the DPP will replace the KMT in the near future as Taiwan's ruling party will be determined by elections in December 1998 for the legislature and the mayors of the two principal cities and a presidential election in the year 2000. DPP leaders have moderated their rhetoric on Taiwan independence as prospects for DPP rule brightened, but none of them has been willing to embrace the KMT's position of the eventual unification of Taiwan with mainland China. Thus, a DPP victory could significantly increase the risk of military conflict in the Taiwan Strait.

The United States has been deeply involved in the Taiwan issue since 1950, when, at the outbreak of the Korean War, it dispatched the 7th Fleet to prevent the People's Liberation Army from invading Taiwan. For twenty years the United States protected the people of Taiwan from mainland attack, provided large amounts of military and economic aid, and supported the government of the ROC as the legitimate representative of all China in the United Nations. In 1979, after establishing diplomatic relations with the PRC and ending diplomatic relations with the ROC, the United States adopted the Taiwan Relations Act (TRA), which stated that any use of force against Taiwan would be of grave concern to the United States; it also bound the U.S. government to provide defensive arms to Taiwan and provided a framework for conducting unofficial relations with the people of Taiwan. Under this unconventional arrangement, economic, academic, personal, and institutional relations have continued to flourish.

Since recognizing the PRC as the only legitimate government of China, the United States has sought to maintain good relations with both the PRC and the people of Taiwan. An appropriate balance has been difficult to maintain, however, because the Tiananmen tragedy created a lasting aversion among the American people to the PRC's rulers. Other differences between Washington and Beijing over human rights, proliferation of missile and nuclear technology, and trade issues have complicated the relationship. Only the difference over Taiwan, however, which PRC leaders consider the most important dispute with the United States, could lead to a military clash.

The purpose of this study is to analyze the evolving relationship between Taiwan and mainland China, evaluating the trends that are drawing them together or keeping them apart, and to make recommendations as to U.S. policies that will promote cross-strait cooperation and diminish the tendency toward confrontation. Will the expansion of people-to-people relations create influential constituencies on both sides of the strait with a growing stake in maintaining a peaceful status quo? Would a successor of President Lee Teng-hui take action in the international arena that would provoke a military response from Beijing? Will the cross-strait dialogue, resumed in 1998, make progress toward agreement on the political relationship between Beijing and Taipei? What U.S. policies toward Beijing and Taipei would minimize the risk of a renewed military confrontation?

This book has been kept short in the hope that it will be more widely read than a longer, more detailed exposition would be. For readers who are unfamiliar with the tortuous course of U.S.-China relations over the past fifty years, Chapter 2 provides a succinct account of how the present relationship among Washington, Beijing and Taipei came about. Those familiar with this background can skim or skip that chapter.

Research for this study included two month-long trips to Beijing, Shanghai, and Taipei, one of them during April 1996, shortly after the military confrontation in the Taiwan Strait. I met with government officials, scholars, journalists, diplomats, businesspeople, and others. I am grateful to all of them for sharing their views with me. I also appreciate the support and assistance provided by the Chiang Ching-kuo Foundation and the 21st Century Foundation in Taipei, the Institute of American Studies of the Chinese Academy of Social Sciences in Beijing, and the Shanghai Institute for International Studies.

Romanizing characters from the Chinese language has been complicated, because the China mainland uses the *pin yin* system, developed by the PRC, while the people of Taiwan generally use the previous standard, the Wade-Giles system. For the names of individuals, places, and organizations on the China mainland, I have used *pin yin*, for those in Taiwan, I have used Wade-Giles, or, in some cases, the individual's own idiosyncratic spelling. For the titles of articles or expressions in Chinese, I have used *pin yin*, whether they originated in the PRC or Taiwan, reserving Wade-Giles for the names of Taiwan publications.

Chapter 1

Cornell Alumnus Attends School Reunion

On June 9, 1995, Lee Teng-hui, age 72, who had received a Ph.D. in agricultural economics from Cornell University in 1968, returned to his alma mater to attend an alumni reunion. Like other distinguished alumni before him, he had been invited to deliver the annual Olin Lecture. He told his audience of four thousand how happy he and his wife were to return to this "beloved campus." He recalled "the long exhausting evenings in the libraries, the soothing and reflective hours at church, the hurried shuttling between classrooms, the evening strolls hand in hand—so many memories of the past have come to mind, filling my heart with joy and gratitude."[1]

Lee's visit, however, was far from being just a sentimental return to his alma mater. As president of the Republic of China on Taiwan (ROC), Lee had been making "private" visits to countries with which Taiwan had no diplomatic relations as a way of enhancing the status of Taiwan in the world community. He had visited Singapore, the Philippines, Indonesia, Thailand, Jordan, and the United Arab Emirates. The People's Republic of China (PRC) protested to the governments of these countries, charging that allowing Lee to visit was contrary to their pledge to recognize only the PRC as the legal government of China, but the various countries fended off the protests with the explanation that the visits had been "unofficial."

For months, Lee's emissaries had pressed for permission for Lee to make a similar "unofficial" visit to the United States. The State Department declined these requests on the grounds that such a visit "would have serious consequences for United States' foreign policy." As late as May 11, 1995, the State Department spokesman declared that "a visit by a person of President Lee's title, whether or not the visit was termed private, would unavoidably be seen by the People's Republic of China

1

as removing an essential element of unofficiality in the U.S.-Taiwan relationship."[2]

It was becoming increasingly difficult, however, for the administration to persuade Congress and the media that the United States should refuse permission for Lee to make a "private" visit. Early in May both houses of Congress passed a sense of the Congress resolution with only one dissenting vote, calling on the president to welcome a private visit by Lee to the United States.[3] The *Washington Post* and the *New York Times* promptly published editorials backing a Lee visit.[4] Members of Congress threatened to attach to other legislation binding provisions that would require the president to admit Lee. Finally, on May 22, 1995, President Clinton reversed long-standing policy and announced that Lee would be issued a visa to attend his alumni reunion at Cornell.

The PRC reacted angrily, summoning the American ambassador and demanding that the United States reverse its decision. "If the United States clings to its erroneous decision to permit the visit on the basis of miscalculation of the situation, it will inevitably cause severe damage to Sino-U.S. relations," the Foreign Ministry spokesman declared.[5] In order to emphasize the damage being done to these relations, the PRC ordered an air force delegation to break off its visit to the United States and return home. It canceled planned June visits by Defense Minister Chi Haotian and State Councilor Li Guixian, suspended talks on controlling missile technology, and postponed a scheduled visit to China by the director of the U.S. Arms Control and Disarmament Agency. The PRC recalled Ambassador Li Daoyu from Washington, giving no indication of when he would return, and delayed approval of the agreement for the newly appointed American ambassador to Beijing, former senator Jim Sasser.

The State Department did its best to avoid lending an official character to Lee's visit. No federal government official met Lee during his stay, although Senators Jesse Helms, Frank Murkowski, and Al D'Amato greeted him during his brief stopover in Syracuse. Cornell University officials referred to him as "President Lee of Taiwan" and did not fly the ROC flag, play the national anthem, or arrange a press conference for him. Lee did not visit Washington on his trip.

The U.S. government's stress on the unofficial character of Lee's visit did little to mollify Beijing, however. PRC spokesmen declared that by admitting Lee, the United States had violated the three communiqués issued by the two governments and had "seriously damaged the foundation of Sino-U.S. relations."[6] As a condition for the improvement of relations, they demanded a statement by Clinton that Lee would not be permitted to visit the United States again.[7] PRC publications in mainland China and Hong Kong attacked the United States in article after article, characterizing the Lee visit as the culmination of a series of hostile acts aimed at preventing the rise of a strong, prosperous, and unified China.[8]

The PRC's denunciations of the United States, while stiff, were less strident than the stream of personal invective launched against Lee Teng-hui. PRC spokesmen and news articles portrayed Lee as a deceitful, untrustworthy figure who claimed to favor the unification of Taiwan with mainland China but, in fact, was trying to move Taiwan, step by step, toward independence. Lee's "pragmatic diplomacy," including his personal visits to foreign countries, aimed at creating "two Chinas" or "one China, one Taiwan," PRC critics declared. They cited his mention of "the Republic of China" seventeen times in his Cornell speech as showing how transparently false was the allegation that his trip to the United States was a private one. Lee was traitorously becoming a puppet of foreigners, they said, in his plot to divide China. One of Beijing's mouthpieces in Hong Kong, the *Wen Wei Po*, quoted "men of insight" in Taiwan to the effect that "Lee's pursuit of Taiwan independence had pushed 21 million people to the brink of disaster."[9]

The PRC did not limit itself to condemnatory rhetoric. On June 16, 1995, the Association for Relations Across the Taiwan Strait (ARATS) notified the Straits Exchange Foundation (SEF) in Taipei that the planned July meeting of the heads of these two quasi-official organizations that had been established to resolve problems in cross-strait, people-to-people relations would have to be postponed. On July 1 the ARATS notified the SEF that regular technical talks between the two sides would also have to be postponed. Subsequent commentaries blamed the Lee visit for causing the suspension of ARATS-SEF talks by poisoning the atmosphere between the two sides.

A still stronger message consisted of a military exercise in late July involving the firing of six surface-to-surface missiles into the sea some eighty-five miles north of Taiwan. Although the PRC's Foreign Ministry spokesman described the firings as normal military exercises, the continuing media attacks on Lee for colluding with elements in the United States to achieve Taiwan's independence left little doubt that the exercises were intended as a warning to Taiwan not to pursue independence. In August the PRC launched a second exercise that included not only the launching of missiles but also artillery firing and joint air-sea combat maneuvers.[10] Although the ROC government urged people to remain calm and sought to play down the threat, the PRC's psychological warfare had considerable impact on Taiwan. The stock market dropped abruptly, and companies and individuals transferred large amounts of capital abroad.[11]

The Presidential Election

The PRC's campaign to warn the people of Taiwan against pro-independence activities did not come to an end with the military exercises and the anti-Lee rhetoric in the summer of 1995. In August the Kuomintang (KMT) nominated Lee Teng-hui as its candidate in the first direct election of a president, to be held in March 1996, in defiance of the admonition by Beijing's *Xinhua* news agency that "To sweep Lee Teng-hui into the trash bin of history is the common historical responsibility of the Chinese on both sides of the Taiwan Strait."[12] Further attacks on Lee were accompanied by another military exercise in late November, not long before the election of the Legislative Yuan on December 2, 1995.

In that election the KMT lost five seats in the 164-member body, squeaking through with only eighty-five seats, a bare majority of three. The Democratic Progressive Party (DPP) made a slight gain from fifty to fifty-four seats, while the New Party, formed of defectors from the KMT, tripled its seats from seven to twenty-one. The New Party, composed mainly of mainlanders, was the most outspoken supporter of unification and opponent of Taiwan independence. Moreover, three of the DPP's leading advocates of independence lost their seats. Consequently, the PRC took comfort from the results. The Foreign Ministry's spokesman asserted that the results showed that the great majority of the people in Taiwan opposed independence.

Beijing's leaders probably were encouraged by the results of the Legislative Yuan election to believe that the missile firings and military exercises had dampened pro-independence sentiment in Taiwan. Hence, they began planning for another series of missile firings and other military exercises before and during the presidential election on March 23, 1996, directed against their bête noire, Lee Teng-hui.

Lee's principal opponent was Peng Ming-min, the DPP candidate, who was an outspoken advocate of independence. Two other contestants were Lin Yang-kang, former head of the Examination Yuan and Chen Lu-an, former head of the Control Yuan. Lin teamed up with Hao Po-tsun, a mainlander with a military background, who had been premier from 1990 to 1993. The New Party candidate withdrew so that the New Party could throw its support to the Lin/Hao slate. Chen withdrew from the KMT, and Lin and Hao, both of whom were KMT vice presidents, were expelled for running against Lee, the KMT-nominated candidate.

During the election campaign, Lin and Chen attacked Lee for having damaged cross-strait relations by his trip to Cornell. They promised to act more prudently in the international arena, to open a dialogue with

Beijing, and to improve cross-strait relations. PRC media in Beijing and Hong Kong continued to excoriate Lee, occasionally quoting Lin, Hao, or Chen's campaign attacks on Lee for obstructing the improvement of cross-strait relations and secretly favoring independence. Such quotes proved a dangerous game for the PRC, however, for they gave Lee backers ammunition with which to blacken Lee's ex-KMT opponents as fostering capitulation to Beijing. To defend themselves against these charges, Lin and Hao had to stress their opposition to early unification with mainland China, defining unification as a long-term objective, a view that differed little from Lee's own stated position.

As in 1995, PRC leaders combined propaganda attacks on Lee with preparations for military actions. They moved additional troops into Fujian province opposite Taiwan, and senior military figures were quoted in the Hong Kong press and by visiting Americans as warning of impending military moves. The most alarming such warning was reported by Chas. W. Freeman, Jr., a former assistant secretary of defense, who told President Clinton's national security adviser, Anthony Lake, in early January 1996 that the People's Liberation Army had prepared plans for a missile attack against Taiwan consisting of one missile a day for thirty days.

ROC government leaders urged the public to remain calm in the face of this disturbing news. The minister of defense discounted Hong Kong reports that the PRC was preparing a massive exercise on Pingtan Island, near ROC-occupied Matsu Island, involving 400,000 troops. ROC intelligence officials described the forthcoming exercise as "routine" and said that it would involve no more than 150,000 troops. In mid-February President Lee visited frontline units on Chinmen (Quemoy) and Premier Lien Chan made a similar trip to Matsu, the other principal offshore island, encouraging the troops to stand firm against PRC threats.

On March 5, 1996, the PRC announced that it would conduct missile exercises between March 8 and March 15, aiming the missiles at splash zones just nineteen miles from Taiwan's northeast coast and twenty-eight miles from Kaohsiung, Taiwan's main port. It warned ships and planes to stay away from the areas during exercises.

On March 8 two surface-to-surface M-9 missiles struck the splash zone near Kaohsiung and one landed in the zone near Keelung. On March 12 the PRC began eight days of live-fire air and sea exercises in a 6,600-square-mile rectangular area off the southeast China coast, extending to the midpoint of the Taiwan Strait. On March 13 the PRC fired another M-9 missile into the splash zone near Kaohsiung. On March 18 the PRC began a week of combined service exercises around Pingtan Island, with an operational area extending to within 11 miles of the ROC-occupied islands of Matsu and Wuchiu. The exercises would not end until after the presidential election on March 23.

U.S. Secretary of State Warren Christopher criticized the PRC's missile firings and military exercises as "unnecessarily risky" and "unnecessarily reckless," warning that belligerent actions against Taiwan would have "grave consequences."[13] President Clinton ordered the USS *Independence* carrier group to move to the vicinity of Taiwan to monitor the PRC exercises and sent a second carrier, the USS *Nimitz*, and escort vessels from the Persian Gulf to arrive in the Taiwan area a few days before the presidential election. The PRC reacted angrily to what it regarded as U.S. intervention in China's domestic affairs, while the ROC welcomed the decision as contributing to peace in the region.

The first direct presidential election in China's history went off smoothly, despite the ominous atmosphere of hostile military exercises in the Taiwan Strait, with 76 percent of eligible voters participating. Lee was elected in a landslide with 54 percent of the vote, Peng received 21 percent, Lin 15 percent and Chen 10 percent.

If PRC leaders hoped to diminish support for Lee by their campaign against him, they did not succeed. On the contrary, a widely held view in Taiwan is that the PRC's offensive actually gained votes for Lee. It is doubtful, however, that Beijing thought that Lee could be defeated, for he had all along held a commanding lead in the polls. The primary PRC objective clearly was to demonstrate to the leaders and people of Taiwan and the United States that it would not hesitate to resort to force if Taiwan sought independence and that it had the necessary military capability to do so. Beijing wanted to warn Lee that if he were to interpret his election as a mandate to step up his activities in the international arena, he could expect renewed military pressures.

Another PRC objective was to repeat the previous summer's demonstration that it could at will, through military exercises, impose economic costs on Taiwan. This time the ROC government had prepared in advance a large fund that it used effectively to prevent any drastic decline in the stock market or in the value of Taiwan's currency. Official intervention was costly, however, by some estimates requiring more than $20 billion.[14] One measure of the flight of capital from Taiwan over the period of the PRC's threatening military exercises was the decline in the government's foreign exchange reserves from a historic peak of $104 billion in June 1995 to $84.76 billion at the end of May 1996.[15]

The PRC's military threats against Taiwan, while giving pause to independence advocates, had side effects that were unanticipated and undesirable from Beijing's viewpoint. Instead of adding credence to Beijing's contention that how it dealt with Taiwan was a purely domestic matter, of no concern to the rest of the world, the threat of force at the time of the presidential election attracted enormous world attention and sympathy to Taiwan. Some 633 media representatives came from 29 countries to report on this dramatic event. Many portrayed it as a victory for democracy in the face of threats from an authoritarian bully. As a KMT official remarked: "Millions of dollars could not have bought this kind of publicity."[16] Senior officials and public figures in countries important to China's modernization, notably Japan, South Korea, and Singapore, expressed concern at the demonstrations of military force in the Taiwan Strait and urged that the differences between Beijing and Taipei be settled peacefully.[17]

Moreover, by sending two carrier task forces to Taiwan, the United States underlined its firmly held view that the Taiwan issue should be resolved peacefully by the Chinese on the two sides of the Taiwan Strait.

Impact of the Military Exercises on U.S.-PRC Relations

The PRC's threatening war games of March 1996 and the dispatch of U.S. carrier task forces in response highlighted the seriousness of the Taiwan issue in U.S.-PRC relations. None of the other disputes between Washington and Beijing on matters such as trade, nonproliferation, or human rights carries the risk of drawing the two nations into a military conflict. Only differences over how Taiwan's future relationship with mainland China should be determined could lead to that dire result. The series of events during the nine months from Lee Teng-hui's visit to Cornell to the arrival of the USS *Nimitz* in Taiwan waters illustrate how misunderstandings and miscalculations on the part of Washington, Beijing, and Taipei could produce consequences that none of them desired.

Lee Teng-hui envisaged a visit to Cornell as the crowning achievement of his personal visits abroad, aimed at enhancing the ROC's international stature. Since the U.S. administration opposed the visit because of the damage it would do to relations with Beijing, Lee mobilized pro-ROC individuals and organizations throughout the country to lobby Congress. He had the KMT sign a three-year, $4.5 million contract with a public relations firm, Cassidy Associates, to contribute to the effort. The lobbying effort was extraordinarily successful, producing a nearly 100 percent vote in favor of Lee's visit.

Lee did not, however, foresee the adverse effects of these actions. He conceded that the PRC's reaction was stronger than he anticipated.[18] Moreover, resort to using Congress to force the president to reverse the administration's position created a backlash against Taiwan among the bureaucrats in the National Security Council and the State Department. They would henceforth be more resistant to persuasion by Taiwan's representatives in the United States to take actions that the Taipei government desired.

In voting for the resolution endorsing Lee's Cornell visit, few members of Congress could have anticipated that their action would lead, ten months later, to the most serious military confrontation between the United States and the PRC since the offshore island crisis of 1958. Members of Congress, like most Americans, saw little reason to oppose a private visit to his alma mater by the president of a friendly, democratic government. It was "no big deal." Few Americans could understand or appreciate why leaders in Beijing would view the approval of Lee's visa as a hostile act, requiring a strong reaction.

Leaders in Beijing also lacked a clear understanding of politics in Taiwan. They could not appreciate the pressures on Lee in a democratic society to take actions to improve the international standing of the ROC on Taiwan in order to counter support for Peng Ming-min's demand for an independent "Republic of Taiwan." They also misinterpreted U.S. opposition to the use of military force to unify Taiwan with mainland China as being an element of a U.S. strategy aimed at preventing China from becoming strong and prosperous.

The misunderstandings and miscalculations of 1995 through 1996 in U.S.-PRC-Taiwan relations are only the latest episode in the long and complicated history of this triangular relationship. A brief sketch of their background in the following chapter will place them in context.

Notes

1. *Free China Review* (August 1995): 4.
2. *New York Times* (May 11, 1995): A6.
3. *Washington Post* (May 10, 1995).
4. *Washington Post* (May 10, 1995); *New York Times* (May 13, 1995).
5. *New York Times* (May 24, 1995); *Beijing Review* (June 12–18, 1995): 18–19.
6. *Beijing Review* (June 19–25, 1995): 22.
7. *New York Times* (July 13, 1995).
8. See, for example, "Where does the United States Really Want to Lead Sino-U.S. Relations?" *Xinhua*, Beijing, June 17, 1995 (Foreign Broadcast Information Service, Daily Report, China [hereafter cited as *FBIS*] [June 19, 1995]: 10–12). Also, "What Has Lee Teng-hui's Visit Brought to Sino-U.S. Relations?" *Liaowang*, July 3, 1995 (*FBIS*, [July 24, 1995]: 3–6).
9. Sept. 7, 1995 *FBIS* (Sept. 20, 1995): 54.
10. *New York Times* (July 24, 1995; August 19, 1995).

11. Capital outflow reached $8.19 billion between July and September, 1995. *China Post*, (Feb. 28, 1996).

12. *Far Eastern Economic Review* (September 7, 1995): 14.

13. *Washington Post* (March 11, 1996).

14. *Far Eastern Economic Review* (March 28, 1996): 58.

15. *Free China Journal* (July 5, 1996): 3.

16. Interview with the author (Taipei, April 1996).

17. John W. Garver, "The International Effect of the Crisis," Chap. 13, in *Face-Off: China, the United States and Taiwan's Democratization* (Seattle, London: The University of Washington Press, 1997), pp. 134–147.

18. Meeting with the author and other American scholars (November 1995).

Chapter 2

Shifting Emphases in
U.S.-PRC-Taiwan Relations

The military confrontation between the United States and the People's
Republic of China (PRC) in March 1996 occurred against the background of the shifting attitudes of Americans and Chinese toward each
other over the previous fifty years. These changing views of the American people and of the Chinese in the two separate polities, mainland
China and Taiwan, that existed after 1949 had strategic, economic, and
values dimensions. They were affected by domestic developments in
each area and by changes in the international community.

The People's Republic of China

Strategic Interests

When Mao Zedong announced the founding of the People's Republic of China in October 1949, he declared that China had at last "stood
up." He was referring to the previous one hundred years during which
China had been weak, divided, and preyed upon by the Western powers and Japan. China was still weak, however, and Mao, fearing attack
from the United States, which had aided Chiang Kai-shek's defeated
Kuomintang regime, signed a security treaty in February 1950 with the
Soviet Union, the main adversary of the United States in the emerging
Cold War. The outbreak of the Korean War in June 1950, the dispatch of
the U.S. 7th Fleet to prevent the People's Liberation Army (PLA) from
conquering Taiwan, and the intervention by Chinese forces in the Korean War marked the beginning of twenty years of hostility between
the United States and the PRC.

Under the slogan "Resist America, Aid Korea," over a million Chi-

11

nese troops fought in Korea, suffering hundreds of thousands of casualties. Communist propaganda painted the United States in the darkest hues, as the leader of the world's imperialist nations, intent on strangling the infant PRC and defeating the world communist movement. Moreover, the United States gave lavish economic and military aid to Chiang Kai-shek, whose battle-cry was "Recover the Mainland"; signed a mutual security treaty with the Republic of China (ROC); and mobilized its friends in the United Nations to exclude the PRC and keep the ROC in the China seat until 1971.

The PRC's strategic alliance with the Soviet Union brought it the Soviet weapons necessary to prevent the U.S.-led UN forces from destroying Communist North Korea. During the mid-1950s, the Soviets also provided the PRC with large amounts of military and economic aid and gave technical training to thousands of Chinese.

But in the late 1950s the alliance broke down. For a decade the PRC faced two dangerous external enemies while going through a desperate domestic political struggle, the Cultural Revolution. After military clashes with the Soviets caused Mao to issue the directive "Dig tunnels deep and store grain everywhere," in preparation for a possible people's war against a Soviet attack, Mao and Zhou Enlai recognized the grave danger to the PRC in maintaining simultaneous hostility to both superpowers. They responded positively to signals from President Richard Nixon and set in motion a strategic rapprochement with the United States as a counter to the Soviet threat.

After Deng Xiaoping became China's paramount leader, the partial rapprochement that had occurred while Mao and the "Gang of Four" were still in power went further. In 1979 the United States established diplomatic relations with the PRC, broke its diplomatic relations and ended the security treaty with the ROC, and agreed to have only nongovernmental relations with the people of Taiwan. Deng's visit to the United States in January 1979 publicized the PRC's new strategic relationship with the United States and set the stage for the PLA's attempt to punish Soviet-aligned Vietnam for its invasion of Cambodia.

The severance of official relations between Washington and Taipei did not, as PRC leaders had hoped, open the way to negotiations with Taipei on the early unification of Taiwan with mainland China. The ROC rebuffed conciliatory PRC proposals for opening trade, travel, and communications across the Taiwan Strait. The United States passed the Taiwan Relations Act (TRA), which provided a framework for unofficial relations between the United States and the people of Taiwan, but, in addition, the act stated that the United States would regard with "grave concern" any attempt at forcible coercion of Taiwan and it provided for the continued supply of defensive arms to Taiwan by the United States. The PRC repeatedly expressed its dissatisfaction with the TRA and stressed that the future of Taiwan remained the most serious issue between the PRC and the United States.

PRC pressure on the United States to halt arms sales to Taiwan produced the August 17, 1982, joint communiqué in which the United States agreed to reduce gradually its arms sales to Taiwan in light of the PRC's statement that its fundamental policy was to strive for a peaceful resolution of the Taiwan question. The PRC has accused the United States of violating the commitments made in this communiqué, particularly in 1992 by the sale to Taiwan of 150 F-16 aircraft.

The collapse of the Soviet Union and the display of U.S. military power in the Gulf War, following closely on the threat to the Chinese Communist Party (CCP) at Tiananmen, made a deep impact on PRC leaders. The strategic configuration of the world had radically changed. The United States was the only remaining superpower, and many Americans were trumpeting victory in the Cold War and the impending demise of the few remaining communist governments.

Taiwan continued to be the principal strategic issue between Beijing and Washington. After the recovery of Hong Kong in 1997 and Macau in 1999, Taiwan will be the only significant piece of Chinese territory over which Beijing has been unable to extend its control. Not only is it a matter of national pride to restore China's territorial integrity by recovering Taiwan, but the island and its 21 million people would be an important strategic asset to China. In the hands of an unfriendly power, it would be a strategic threat. Japan had demonstrated the strategic value of the island in World War II, when it became a crucial base supporting Japan's military drive into Southeast Asia.

During the 1990s the view gained currency among strategic thinkers in the PRC that the United States was bent on preserving its hegemony over East Asia by containing China, preventing it from becoming a strong and prosperous nation. An element in this presumed policy of containment was to prevent the unification of Taiwan with the PRC. Those who held this view pointed to U.S. policies since 1949 aimed at keeping Taiwan separate from the Chinese motherland. Not only did some Americans express concern about an emerging "China threat" and openly advocate a policy of containment, but others, even members of the U.S. Congress, urged the U.S. government to support UN membership for Taiwan.

Political change in Taiwan added to the uneasiness felt in the PRC over the future of Taiwan. The Democratic Progressive Party (DPP), which held close to one-third of the seats in the Legislative Yuan, advocated an independent "Republic of Taiwan." After Lee Teng-hui succeeded to the presidency in 1988, he embarked on a program of "pragmatic diplomacy" in which he and other high-ranking officials made unofficial but highly visible trips to countries that had diplomatic relations with the PRC. The ruling KMT party joined the DPP in a high-decibel campaign to seek participation for Taiwan in the United Nations.

Thus, in spite of the rapid growth of economic ties between Taiwan and mainland China, the PRC feared that under Lee Teng-hui Taiwan was moving, step by step, toward independence. Lee's visit to Cornell and the dispatch of U.S. warships to the Taiwan area in March 1996 confirmed in the minds of many Chinese that the United States had been, and still was, determined that Taiwan would be its "unsinkable aircraft carrier."

Latent animosity toward Japan among Chinese, deeply embedded by Japan's invasion of China during the 1930s and 1940s, has nourished suspicion of Japan's military build-up and strategic intentions. Concern existed that the Japanese might share the presumed U.S. strategy of keeping Taiwan out of the PRC's control. PRC leaders were aware that the Japanese had strong links with the people of Taiwan based on the previous colonial relationship, the large Japanese trade and investment in Taiwan, and Taiwan's dependence on Japan for industrial technology.

Lee Teng-hui's Japan connections intensified Chinese suspicions of Japan's intentions. Lee graduated from Kyoto University and speaks fluent Japanese. PRC commentators frequently cited Lee's lengthy interview in Japanese with *Shukan Asahi* correspondent Ryotaro Shiba, in April 1994 as revealing Lee's pro-Japanese and pro-independence leanings.[1] Lee has made no secret of his wish to follow up his Cornell visit with a visit to his alma mater in Japan. The PRC noted with concern President Clinton's April 1996 trip to Japan to reinvigorate the U.S.-Japan alliance in the immediate aftermath of the dispatch of a Japan-based aircraft carrier to the Taiwan region.

Economic Interests

When the PRC was founded, China was an immense, but poor and backward, country, just beginning to recover from many years of debilitating war. Almost immediately, it plunged into the Korean conflict, provoking an economic embargo by the Western powers and Japan and further delaying economic recovery. The Soviet Union made a substantial contribution to the industrialization of China, but by 1960 political differences caused Moscow to end its economic and military aid and withdraw its advisers.

The PRC was on its own, abandoned by its Soviet "elder brother" and denied a relationship with the other superpower, which continued its economic embargo against China through the 1960s. In 1958 Mao launched the ill-fated Great Leap Forward, which, along with several years of bad harvests, did severe damage to the Chinese economy. In the 1960s and early 1970s China was convulsed by the Cultural Revolution. It followed an inward-looking economic policy, declining to take advantage of the rapid growth of world trade during this period. Consequently, by the 1970s, China's rate of economic growth fell far behind that of the export-oriented four little dragons of East Asia: South Korea, Taiwan, Hong Kong, and Singapore.

Only after Deng Xiaoping launched a radical policy of economic reform and opening to the outside in 1978 did China shake off its lethargy. It soon became the fastest growing country in the world, with real GNP expanding at over 9 percent annually from 1978 through 1993.[2] China became a magnet for foreign direct investment. Through 1993 the cumulative total of foreign direct investment actually undertaken reached $60 billion and the cumulative value of foreign investment contracts exceeded $220 billion.[3] By 1996 China had become the largest recipient of World Bank loans, averaging $3 billion a year in recent years and totaling over $25 billion.[4]

After China began its economic opening to the outside, the United States has become an increasingly important partner, since 1992 taking one-third of China's exports and transferring advanced technological skills, such as in the commercial aircraft industry. American firms became the second or third largest suppliers of capital. Thus, the PRC had an important economic interest in good relations with the United States.

Hong Kong has been the largest investor in mainland China, supplying around 60 percent of foreign direct investment. Since 1987 Taiwan entrepreneurs have also invested sizeable amounts, estimated at about $30 billion from some 30,000 firms.

The overriding mission for Chinese leaders was to press ahead with economic modernization so that China could catch up with Japan and the West and become a powerful and prosperous nation, assuming again its proper place in the world community. Capital, technology, and managerial and marketing skills provided by Taiwan entrepreneurs contributed to the achievement of this goal. The growing economic interaction also linked Taiwan more firmly to the China mainland and improved the prospects for unification.

Beijing's economic interest in modernization and its strategic interest in the unification of Taiwan with the mainland were consistent, in the sense that a unified China would be more modern and powerful than the PRC is today. Resources devoted by Beijing and Taipei to confronting each other could be more productively employed. But if the PRC were compelled to resort to force to prevent Taiwan independence, it would be defending its strategic interests at a high cost in terms of its economic interests in relations with Taiwan, the United States, and Japan.

Values

During Mao's lifetime, the values pushed assiduously by the Chinese Communist Party (CCP) were those of Marxism-Leninism, as modified through the prism of Mao Zedong thought. The turmoil of the Cultural Revolution, however, so damaged the credibility of the CCP that party leaders ever since have been groping for an official ideology that people would accept. Deng's pragmatism, with his slogans "Seek truth from facts," "To get rich is glorious," and "It doesn't matter whether a cat is black or white so long as it catches mice," made possible the shift to a market economy and opening to the outside. Calling the reform policies "socialism with Chinese characteristics" provided a description that differentiated these policies from Marxism-Leninism but did not provide a firm ideological foundation.

People in general, to the extent that they paid attention to matters beyond personal and family affairs, were motivated primarily by desires for political stability, economic growth, and national resurgence. Stability required avoiding the political fanaticism that led to the breakdown of order during the Cultural Revolution. Rapid economic growth has spread the gains widely enough to limit dissatisfaction with Communist Party rule, but if economic growth were to slow too much or if inflation were to get out of hand, discontent would spread among increasing numbers who were unable to share in economic gains. Finally, national resurgence, a feeling that China would soon be resuming its proper role as a great power, could be readily stimulated by the leadership as a replacement for the lost ideological vision of a communist paradise. However, stirring up nationalistic feelings by appealing to latent xenophobia could make it more difficult to secure the cooperation needed from the United States, Japan, and Europe to achieve China's objectives.

The PRC's political leaders had the uneasy feeling that the lack of a generally accepted official ideology left people open to being misled by ideas coming from outside China. Opening to the outside, which was essential to economic growth, left the door open to undesirable intellectual breezes. Periodic campaigns against "spiritual pollution" did not suffice to keep these out. In the era of radio, television, the fax machine, and the Worldwide Web, ideas were hard to exclude. Nevertheless, the attempt to formulate and establish a "Chinese spiritual civilization" went forward, an effort to modernize China while preserving those values that would contribute to perpetuating the rule of the Chinese Communist Party.

The United States

Strategic Interests

In 1949, when the PRC defeated KMT forces in mainland China and declared its intention to lean to the Soviet side in the emerging Cold War, the post–World War II strategy of the United States in East Asia, based on collaboration with a friendly China, was shattered. Washington had to shift quickly to make Japan the linchpin of its regional strategy. U.S. leaders sought ways to keep Taiwan from falling into Chinese Communist hands, but the Joint Chiefs of Staff were unwilling to commit U.S. forces to the defense of Taiwan.[5] Hence, in January 1950 President Harry Truman declared that the United States had no intention of interfering with its armed forces or providing military aid and advice to the ROC. But the outbreak of the Korean War caused Truman to reverse his position and order the U.S. 7th Fleet to protect Taiwan and to prevent any attempt by the ROC to attack the mainland. China's alliance with the Soviet Union and Chinese military intervention in the Korean War convinced most Americans that the PRC was serving Soviet purposes in furthering the spread of international communism. Communist rebellions in French Indochina and other countries of Southeast Asia, backed by the Sino-Soviet bloc, strengthened this view.

It was difficult for the United States to take immediate strategic advantage of the fracturing of the Sino-Soviet alliance in the 1960s, for both countries were aiding North Vietnam in its conflict with South Vietnam and the United States. The Cultural Revolution in China also ruled out for several years any radical foreign policy initiatives by Beijing. By 1971, however, American public opinion had become more amenable to the establishment of relations with Beijing, it was no longer possible to exclude the PRC from the United Nations, and both Washington and Beijing saw advantages in a rapprochement to strengthen their respective positions against the Soviet Union. The PRC was increasingly conscious of a Soviet threat after the August 1968 invasion of Czechoslovakia and Sino-Soviet military clashes on the border. The United States saw the rapprochement with China as useful in the context of negotiations with Hanoi and the withdrawal of U.S. forces from Vietnam.

During the twenty-two years since 1949, the American people had become accustomed to viewing the ROC on Taiwan as a partner in the Cold War. Innumerable close governmental, institutional, economic, and personal bonds had developed by 1971. It would not be possible for the United States to turn its back on Taiwan as President Truman had done in 1950.

Although the United States had not established a permanent military base on Taiwan, the island was useful during the Vietnam War. It provided a base for logistical aircraft supporting U.S. military operations in Vietnam, it served as a popular rest and recreation site for U.S. troops from Vietnam, and it had the best repair facilities in East Asia, outside of Japan, for overhauling U.S. fighter aircraft, tanks, and personnel carriers. Official statements frequently mentioned the ROC on Taiwan as making up part of the chain of alliances in the western Pacific that served to contain Soviet and Chinese expansionism.

The common strategic interest of the United States and China in cooperating against the Soviet Union facilitated the compromise reached in normalizing diplomatic relations with Beijing in 1979 and providing for unofficial relations between the United States and the people of Taiwan. Both Washington and Beijing were deeply concerned with Soviet aid to Vietnam in the occupation of Cambodia and the Soviet occupation of Afghanistan. The U.S. Congress and the American people in general approved of the normalization of relations with Beijing but also supported the concern expressed in the TRA with the future security of Taiwan.

Throughout the 1980s Taiwan continued to be the primary issue between Washington and Beijing. Some influential members of Congress attacked the 1982 agreement on reducing arms sales to Taiwan as being contrary to the TRA's commitment to furnish Taiwan with defensive arms. The PRC also criticized the U.S. government for not strictly adhering to the letter and spirit of that agreement. Meanwhile, the governments of the United States and Taiwan were learning to adjust to unofficial relations, and bonds of all kinds continued to grow stronger.

Despite the shared strategic interest of the United States and the PRC in countering the Soviet Union, the U.S. government and the American people were reluctant to see the people of Taiwan forced to submit to control by the communist government in Beijing. The U.S. government followed a "two-track" policy in dealing with Beijing and Taipei, taking the position that the future of Taiwan should be decided by the people on the two sides of the Taiwan Strait. The United States would not become involved in mediating their differences; its only concern was that the solution be arrived at peacefully.

The year 1989 brought a radical change in American views of China.

The increasingly favorable view, encouraged by economic reforms and the resulting rapid economic growth, was abruptly reversed by the appalling television shots of troops firing on unarmed civilians around Tiananmen square. This blow to U.S.-PRC relations was soon followed by the collapse of the Soviet Union, which eliminated the principal rationale for promoting strategic cooperation with the PRC. In the debate that ensued in the United States concerning a new strategic concept to replace that which prevailed during the Cold War, a school of thought emerged that saw China as a rising power, likely to be expansionist and therefore needing to be contained. The U.S. government did not accept the containment thesis but recognized the growing importance of China in the world and the need for policies that would help to integrate it constructively into the world community.

While American views of the PRC were becoming more critical, not only because of Tiananmen but also because of more recent violations of human rights and disputes over trade and the proliferation of weapons of mass destruction, views of Taiwan were becoming more favorable. Mutually beneficial trade relations grew, trade disputes were resolved by pragmatic compromises, and, most impressive of all, over a period of ten years the authoritarian one-party political system was transformed into a multi-party democratic system, a sharp contrast with communist rule on the mainland.

Economic Interests

During the first two decades after 1949, the United States maintained that an economic embargo against the PRC and Taiwan was an economic burden rather than an asset because of economic and military aid programs. The U.S. government justified expenditures in support of Taiwan as part of the cost of defending the free world against communist expansionism.

After the establishment of relations with Beijing, the United States removed its economic embargo, but trade and investment remained small until the PRC entered its period of rapid growth after 1978. The lure of the immense China market fascinated American entrepreneurs. Multinational corporations increasingly felt a need to establish a presence in China in order to avoid being preempted by Japanese or European competitors, even though the difficulties of doing business in China often meant that years would pass before substantial profits could be expected. Bilateral trade zoomed from $1.1 billion in 1978 to $57.3 billion in 1995, with a U.S. deficit of $33.9 billion.[6] Cumulative investments by U.S. firms made them the first or second largest foreign investors during the 1990s (excluding Hong Kong and Taiwan).

Although China became the sixth largest trading partner of the United States and the appeal of economic relations with China's huge and rapidly growing economy remained strong, Americans differed widely in evaluating the U.S. economic interest in China. Some stressed the problems in trade with China: barriers to American exports that helped create the rising trade deficit, widespread piracy of American intellectual property, and mislabeling of Chinese-made goods as products of other countries in order to avoid quotas. Others stressed the growing market in China for U.S. agricultural products and commercial aircraft and the potential for much greater exports as the Chinese economy continued to grow.

The most severe strain in U.S.-China trade relations arose after the Tiananmen shootings highlighted the PRC's suppression of human rights. Many members of Congress, both Democratic and Republican, sought to overturn the president's annual decision required by the Jackson-Vanik Amendment to the 1974 Trade Act to continue most-favored-nation (MFN) treatment for China, arguing that threatening to withdraw MFN treatment would compel Chinese leaders to improve their treatment of human rights. Opponents of such an attempt to exert pressure on PRC leaders argued that it would not achieve its purpose. Moreover, Chinese retaliation to the withdrawal of MFN treatment would sharply reduce U.S. exports to the PRC. Hong Kong and Taiwan would also suffer severely, because the thousands of factories in China owned by their entrepreneurs could no longer sell their products in the United States.

By the autumn of 1996 the forces opposed to using withdrawal of MFN status as a cudgel to exact better adherence to human rights standards in China had grown stronger. The concept that MFN status is not a special privilege but is the treatment extended to nearly all of our trading partners was becoming better understood. In 1994 the Clinton administration had explicitly delinked the decision on MFN treatment from human rights concerns. The view was gaining ground that expanding foreign trade and investment in China would contribute to economic growth and China's opening to the outside world, which would, in the long run, bring about desirable political reform. Some scholars and members of Congress were recommending a change in the Jackson-Vanik Amendment so that China would be treated like our other principal trading partners rather than be subjected to the recurring annual uncertainty as to whether its MFN status would be continued.[7]

U.S. economic interests in Taiwan also grew substantially during the 1980s and 1990s, although less rapidly than U.S.-PRC trade. In 1995 two-way trade was $48.3 billion compared to U.S.-PRC trade of $57.3

billion. The PRC was the sixth largest trading partner of the United States and Taiwan was the eighth largest. Taiwan, however, was a more important buyer of U.S. goods, as the U.S. deficit in trade with Taiwan was only $9.7 billion compared to $33.9 billion for the PRC, second only to the U.S. deficit in trade with Japan. Still, the prospects for growth in U.S. exports to China's huge market far exceeded prospects for U.S. exports to Taiwan.

Values

Americans had historically developed a fascination with China and a sympathy for the Chinese people. The missionary impulse was strong; Americans contributed generously to the support of American missionaries in China and the establishment of universities and medical schools. The Chinese were poor, were badly governed, and needed American help. U.S. opposition to Japanese aggression against China, compounded by Japan's invasion of French Indochina in 1940, led to U.S. involvement in World War II.

After the advent of the Cold War, the Chinese Communist victory, and the formation of the Sino-Soviet bloc, American attitudes toward China were dominated for many years by anticommunism. Participation in wars in Korea and Vietnam convinced most Americans that the leaders of China and the Soviet Union were promoting a global movement that threatened the American way of life.

Americans who were interested in China but cut off from contact with people on the China mainland shifted their attention to the Chinese on Taiwan. Although American disillusionment with the Chiang Kai-shek regime was profound, that government's firm commitment to anticommunism still made it a useful ally in the global struggle. Private Americans developed relations with educational institutions in Taiwan, and Christian denominations, denied access to mainland China, sent numerous missionaries to Taiwan. Economic aid, while justified officially as a contribution to the defense of the free world against communism, also appealed to Americans' desire to benefit Chinese. Taiwan's rapid economic growth and rise in living standards demonstrated that the American contribution had been put to good use.

In the anticommunist struggle, cooperation with an authoritarian ruler such as Chiang Kai-shek made it difficult to promote in Taiwan the other values prized by Americans: democracy and the protection of human rights. Certain members of Congress and some private Americans publicly criticized the Chiang Kai-shek regime's repressive political system, but the U.S. government felt constrained by the need to gain maximum cooperation from an ally in a global contest. Nevertheless, in a broad sense, American influence on the people of Taiwan through a multiplicity of channels over a forty-year period undoubtedly helped to create the conditions that made possible the emergence of a democratic political system in Taiwan in the 1990s.[8]

Although many Americans recognized the need for strategic and economic cooperation with the PRC, and others, for a time, held excessively romantic ideas about that country, a strong undercurrent of animosity toward the communist government in Beijing remained. After the demise of the Soviet Union, confidence grew that the Beijing regime would be supplanted by a democratic system. Americans differed widely in their judgments as to how long that might take and what the United States should do to bring it about, but most agreed that it would occur sooner or later. The growing interaction between institutions and individuals in China and the United States, particularly the tens of thousands of young Chinese pursuing advanced degrees in American universities, suggested that the process that encouraged the transition to democracy in Taiwan was already under way with respect to the PRC, but it would likely require at least several decades to come to fruition.

China policy has at times become the subject of intense political debate in the United States. In the early 1950s Republicans attacked the Truman administration for "having lost China." During the Eisenhower administration in the 1950s, policies toward the offshore islands occupied by ROC forces provoked argument both within and outside the administration. In this period differences were over tactics, not over the weight to give American values, as there was a broad consensus on anticommunism and the need to contain China.

After Tiananmen, and especially after the collapse of the Soviet Union, the debate focused heavily on values: whether U.S. policy should be dominated by an effort to improve the treatment of human rights in China, with U.S. strategic and economic concerns given a lesser priority. Some Democrats and Republicans have drawn on the public dislike of political repression in the PRC to gain political advantage by lambasting a president from the rival party for being too soft on the Chinese Communists.

Taiwan

Strategic Interests

Taiwan is too small to be a major player in big-power maneuvering in the Asia-Pacific region. It could only survive if it were allied to a big power, and it had little choice but to cast its lot with the United States early in the Cold War. Chiang Kai-shek and Chiang Ching-kuo played their few cards well, gaining protection for Taiwan and building up its economic and military strength. With U.S. backing the ROC clung to the China seat in the United Nations for twenty-two years as the legitimate representative of China.

During the 1970s the ROC suffered two heavy blows: the loss of the UN seat in 1971 and the loss of diplomatic relations and the security treaty with the United States in 1979. Encouraged, however, by the concern expressed for Taiwan's security in the Taiwan Relations Act (TRA), ROC authorities redoubled their efforts to cement relations with the United States. They tried to compensate for their lack of access to top executive branch officials by cultivating members of Congress and their staff, governors and members of state legislatures, officials of important U.S. cities, and key media decision makers. They invited large numbers of national and local political figures to visit Taiwan (Bill Clinton made four visits while governor of Arkansas). They strengthened Taiwan's links with American universities and think-tanks, sponsored a large number of academic conferences at which Taiwan's problems were sympathetically discussed, and hired public relations firms to spread favorable publicity about Taiwan and to lobby members of Congress.

Taiwan's ability to influence Americans favorably was greatly facilitated by the fact that tens of thousands of Taiwan's elite—politicians, bureaucrats, business leaders, educators, scientists, engineers, journalists, and others—received graduate educations in American universities. Many had held professional positions in the United States before returning to Taiwan.

Selling Taiwan to Americans was made easier by Taiwan's economic success and by the transformation of its political system into a multiparty democracy, which made a highly favorable impression in the United States. The contrast with the political repression under the communist government in Beijing was striking. This contrast and the ROC's superior public relations skills, exercised over many years, accounted in large measure for the nearly unanimous vote in the U.S. Congress in favor of Lee Teng-hui's Cornell visit.

The ability of the ROC government to retain the support of the United States was complicated by domestic politics in Taiwan. The principal difference between the KMT and the DPP became whether to stand for the eventual unification of Taiwan with mainland China or to advocate the independence of Taiwan. The KMT's adherence to a "one China" policy, while interpreted differently from the PRC's "one China" policy, enabled the United States to maintain a declaratory policy regarding the future of Taiwan that did not clash with that of the PRC.

Beginning in 1993, DPP pressure caused the ROC government to join in a campaign to gain a seat for Taiwan in the United Nations, a campaign that the PRC views as a step toward an independent Taiwan and that the U.S. government declined to support. Through a variety of offices and organizations in the United States, the DPP worked assiduously to gain support among Americans for Taiwan's independence. The U.S. government, however, unwilling to risk being drawn into a military conflict with the PRC over Taiwan and conscious of its strategic and economic interests in good relations with the PRC, would not back the establishment of an independent state of Taiwan.

The large majority given Lee Teng-hui in the presidential election of March 1996 and the results of public opinion polls indicated that the bulk of the people on Taiwan preferred the status quo of de facto independence to early unification with the PRC or risking war by declaring formal independence. The ROC government thus was in a strong position to resist DPP pressures for independence and to maintain the support required from the United States to safeguard its security. The dispatch of U.S. carriers to the Taiwan area in March 1996 gave reassurance that the United States firmly opposed any attempt to subdue Taiwan by force.

The ROC, in addition to cementing its links with the United States, has also sought to develop mutually beneficial interaction with the PRC since 1987, as a means of strengthening the security of Taiwan. Growing travel, trade, and investment across the Taiwan Strait, which will be discussed in detail in a subsequent chapter, improved mutual understanding, created sizeable interest groups on both sides with a stake in peace in the strait, and contributed to reduced tension. ROC leaders recognized that they could not rely excessively on U.S. support but had to work hard to create a manageable relationship with their powerful neighbor. They also understood that the better the relationship between Taipei and Beijing, the easier it would be for the United States to maintain satisfactory relations with both centers of power.

ROC leaders knew that the United States was the only nation that had the power and will to enable Taiwan to survive as a de facto sovereign state. Nevertheless, they sought to strengthen relations as much as possible with other countries as well, believing that sympathy and moral support from the international community would help Taiwan resist pressures from the PRC. By the 1990s the ROC had diplomatic relations with only about thirty countries, mainly small states in Africa and Central America. Consequently, with those countries that had diplomatic relations with the PRC, the ROC had to rely primarily on its extensive and important economic links.

The ROC did not, however, abandon its efforts to retain and to expand where possible its diplomatic and official relationships. In an intensified campaign dubbed "pragmatic diplomacy," the ROC induced some small countries to switch their diplomatic relations from Beijing to Taipei and strove to heighten its official profile elsewhere through "private" overseas visits by President Lee Teng-hui and other senior officials. The PRC condemned these actions as being contrary to the ROC's professed commitment to "one China" and believed they were actually intended to promote Taiwan independence rather than unification. The hostile PRC reaction raised a question that was debated during the presidential election campaign: In terms of Taiwan's security, can closer symbolic ties with foreign countries counterbalance the increased risk of PRC military action against Taiwan and the adverse impact on the effort to strengthen mutually beneficial ties with the PRC?

Economic Interests

In 1949 when the Nationalist government moved to Taiwan, the island's economy was in bad shape. Resources had been shipped to the mainland to support the war effort, inflation was raging, and the island economy had to absorb nearly two million refugees from the mainland into its population of six million. In 1952 the per capita GNP was only $196. By 1960, however, helped by U.S. military protection and economic aid averaging $100 million annually, the economy stabilized and the foundation had been prepared for an economic takeoff.

During the 1960s and 1970s Taiwan's export-oriented economy grew very rapidly, making it possible to phase out U.S. economic aid in 1965. Rapid growth continued during the 1980s, despite the loss of diplomatic relations with the United States, Taiwan's principal export market. During the first half of the 1990s, the average annual economic growth rate slowed to 6.5 percent, but even so by 1995 Taiwan's per capita GNP exceeded $12,400.[9]

The structure of Taiwan's economy changed radically between 1950 and 1995. Its primarily agricultural economy soon became a center of light industry, which was later supplemented by heavy industry, such as steel production, shipbuilding and petrochemicals. In recent years it has become one of the world's leading manufacturers of information technology products, such as computers, scanners, and waferchips. By 1995 services accounted for 60 percent of the gross domestic product.

Moreover, Taiwan was a major capital exporter, with at least $20 billion invested in mainland China and a similar amount in Southeast Asia.[10]

Taiwan's leaders relied on its strong economy to bolster its ability to resist PRC pressure. Through its rapid growth, Taiwan achieved worldwide renown as one of East Asia's "four little dragons." It became the fourteenth largest trading nation in the world. Its position in 1995 as the eighth largest trading partner of the United States and the sixth largest market for U.S. exports fortified U.S. interest in the security of Taiwan. As the second largest investor in mainland China and the provider of valued technology and managerial and marketing skills, Taiwan gave the PRC an incentive to resolve differences with the government in Taiwan by peaceful means rather than by force.

Taiwan's leaders were able to point to its large and growing economy to justify its membership in the Asian Development Bank, the Asia-Pacific Cooperation group (APEC), and its application to join the World Trade Organization. In 1995 they undertook extensive reform of the laws and regulations governing the economy to make Taiwan more attractive to transnational corporations as an Asia-Pacific regional operations center.

The maintenance of a healthy economy made possible gradual, nonviolent political change, which led ultimately to the transformation of an authoritarian political system into a democracy. In addition, Taiwan's leaders regarded a strong, innovative economy as an essential foundation from which to eventually negotiate a satisfactory long-term political relationship with the PRC.

Leading entrepreneurs in Taiwan recognized that Taiwan's future was becoming increasingly linked to opportunities on the China mainland. By 1996 it appeared likely that Taiwan's combined exports to Hong Kong and mainland China would soon surpass its exports to the United States. The extension of PRC sovereignty over Hong Kong on June 30, 1997, would give Beijing greater influence over Taiwan's trade with Hong Kong. Government officials expressed concern that Taiwan's economy was becoming too dependent on trade with the PRC, but some analysts in Taiwan took the view that the degree of economic *interdependence* between the two areas would limit the risk of political interference by Beijing with Taiwan's mainland trade and investment.

Values

Under Chiang Kai-shek and Chiang Ching-kuo, when Chinese from the mainland dominated the KMT, the government, and the military, Sun Yat-sen's *San Min Chu Yi* (Three Principles of the People) was the officially promulgated ideology. Sun recommended giving a high pri-

ority to economic modernization, carrying out land reform, and promoting foreign investment and foreign trade. These recommendations
became basic elements in the policy followed in Taiwan. Most important in Sun's ideology was his commitment to a democratic system in
China, following a period of "political tutelage" by the KMT, during
which people would be educated and prepared for democracy. Thus,
the two Chiangs had to justify their departures from democratic practices as wartime expedients. The goal of democratization expressed in
the *San Min Chu Yi* became a useful instrument for those pressing for
political reform in Taiwan.

The culmination of the reform process in the popular election of Lee
Teng-hui in March 1996 had a powerful effect on the view that the people of Taiwan had of themselves. They felt that Taiwan had aligned itself with the wave of democratization that swept the world after the
collapse of communism in the Soviet Union and eastern Europe. They
believed that Taiwan had positioned itself to receive stronger backing
from the United States and other democracies against the threat posed
by the last remaining large communist power. Selection of their leader
by popular vote also strengthened the widely held view that Taiwan
was a de facto sovereign state, deserving of recognition by other nations.

Throughout the existence of the Republic of China on Taiwan, anticommunism had been a central feature of its ideology. The KMT condemned communism as an alien ideology imported into China from
the Soviet Union, and any manifestation of sympathy with communism was prohibited on Taiwan. Although public support of communist ideology in the PRC was greatly weakened by the Cultural Revolution, followed by the introduction of a market economy and the
opening to the outside, the fact that the Chinese Communist Party continued to profess adherence to the doctrine and threatened the use of
force against Taiwan ensured that the people of Taiwan would remain
firmly anticommunist. Moreover, the collapse of communism elsewhere in the world and Taiwan's impressive lead over the PRC in
building a modern society were striking demonstrations that communism had little to offer.

Rule over Taiwan by people from the China mainland (mainlanders)
caused resentment among the native Taiwanese, who constituted 85
percent of Taiwan's population. Resentment was greatly intensified by
the brutal suppression of a Taiwanese uprising in 1947. The Taiwanese,
even though they were descendants of earlier immigrants from Fujian
and Guangdong, had lived under Japanese colonial rule for fifty years
and had weaker ties with the mainland than the more recent arrivals.
These differences were reflected in the political controversy between

advocates of unification with mainland China and advocates of Taiwan independence. The former tended to regard themselves as Chinese first, members of a community of people sharing Chinese language and culture, centered in mainland China, and only secondarily as Taiwanese. The latter saw themselves first as citizens of Taiwan, which had been separated from mainland China for nearly one hundred years and had developed a distinctive language and culture. Their identification with mainland Chinese language and culture was secondary. The influence of the latter group increased as the generation that came over from the mainland in 1949 died off and the Taiwanese, under the leadership of Lee Teng-hui, became the dominant faction in the KMT and also constituted the chief opposition party.

Differences over identity were subordinated, however, to a common interest in the continued freedom of Taiwan's people to manage their own affairs in the world. Hence, whether mainlanders or Taiwanese, the great majority opposed either unification or independence in the foreseeable future in a pragmatic effort to avoid either being absorbed into or attacked by the PRC.

Notes

1. See, for example, article transmitted by *Xinhua* domestic service, August 23, 1995 (*FBIS* [August 25, 1995]: 88). Text of Lee's interview published in Taipei's *Tzuli Choupao* (*Independence Post Weekly* [May 13, 1994]). English translation in *Joint Publications Research Service* (JPRS-China [May 13, 1994], JPRS-CAR-040).

2. Nicholas Lardy, *China in the World Economy* (Washington, D.C.: Institute for International Economics, 1994) p. 3.

3. Lardy, p. 64.

4. Pieter Botelier, Director, Beijing Office, World Bank.

5. For a detailed discussion of this critical period, see David M. Finkelstein, *Washington's Taiwan Dilemma: From Abandonment to Salvation, 1949–1950* (Fairfax, VA: George Mason University Press, 1993).

6. The 1978 figure is from Lardy, p. 74. The 1995 figures are from *Far Eastern Economic Review* (September 5, 1996): 61. According to Lardy's analysis, official U.S. figures overstate the bilateral U.S. trade deficit with China by one-third because of the failure to take account of Hong Kong's role in the transshipment of goods to and from China (Lardy, p. 77).

7. For recommendations favoring removal of the requirement for annual approval of MFN treatment of China, see A. Doak Barnett and others, *Developing a Peaceful, Stable and Cooperative Relationship with China* (A National Committee on American Foreign Policy Report, July 1996) p. 13; Representative Lee Hamilton, Speech to Council on Foreign Relations (May 23, 1996), pp. 9–10;

Kim R. Holmes and Thomas G. Moore, eds., *Restoring American Leadership* (Washington, D. C.: Heritage Foundation, 1996) pp. 62–63.

  8. Cheng-yi Lin, "The U.S. Factor in Taiwan's Political Development," in Jaw-Ling Joanne Chang, ed., *ROC-US Relations 1979–1989* (Taipei: Academia Sinica, 1991), pp. 125–167.

  9. (Taipei), Council for Economic Planning and Development, *Taiwan Statistical Data Book, 1996*, p. 1.

  10. Accurate figures on overseas investments by Taiwan firms are not available, because much investment comes from funds held overseas and is not always reported to the government.

Chapter 3

The Political Impasse

During the nine months following Lee Teng-hui's fateful Cornell visit, personal attacks on Lee and missile exercises near Taiwan took precedence over the PRC's campaign to draw the people of Taiwan closer through economic and cultural interchange. Beijing authorities tried to minimize the adverse impact on cross-strait trade and investment by sending Tang Shubei, the vice chairman of the Association for Relations Across the Taiwan Strait (ARATS), on a tour of south China to assure worried Taiwanese businessmen that the heightened political tension would not affect economic relations. It was obvious, however, that Beijing's leaders were willing, if necessary, to pay a significant price in damage to the cross-strait economic relationship in order to check what they saw as Lee Teng-hui's dangerous tendency to move Taiwan, step by step, toward independence.

The nine-month confrontation had a sobering effect on both sides. Personal attacks on Lee diminished; the election had demonstrated that the man with whom the PRC would have to deal for the next four years had a solid base of support among the people of Taiwan. During the remainder of the year, Lee did not take any additional private journeys abroad. Each side waited for the other side to make the first move to ease political tension. When the year ended, each had made some moves in this international chess game, but the fundamental political impasse was little changed. The basic positions remained as they had been formally defined in 1993–1994.

Positions of the Two Governments and the Opposition Party in Taiwan

The PRC Position[1]

1. There is only one China and Taiwan is a province of China.
2. Taiwan should be reunified with mainland China as a "special ad-

31

ministrative region," with its own political and economic system and its own armed forces. Under the "one country, two systems" concept, it will be granted extensive autonomy, more than that granted to the Hong Kong special administrative region.

3. The PRC encourages expansion of economic, personal, and institutional interchange between Taiwan and mainland China and urges early opening of direct communication, travel, and shipping (in brief, referred to as the "three links").

4. The PRC wants negotiations to end the state of hostility between the two sides and bring about reunification.

5. Only the PRC has the right to represent China, including Taiwan, in international affairs.

6. The PRC opposes diplomatic or official relations between Taiwan and countries with which the PRC has diplomatic relations, but it does not object to unofficial economic and cultural relations between Taiwan and those countries.

7. The PRC opposes Taiwan's participation as a separate nation-state in intergovernmental organizations of which only states can be members.

8. The PRC opposes the sale of arms to Taiwan by any state having diplomatic relations with the PRC.

9. PRC consent must be obtained before any state that has diplomatic relations with the PRC establishes aviation services to Taiwan.

10. The PRC reserves to right to use military force to prevent the establishment of an independent state of Taiwan. The refusal to renounce force is not aimed at compatriots in Taiwan, but at foreign forces working to bring about Taiwan independence.

The ROC Position[2]

1. There is only one China, but since 1949 China has been divided into two separate political entities.

2. The ROC has been a sovereign, independent state since 1912, but since 1949 has consisted of only Taiwan, Penghu and the offshore islands. It has never been a part of the PRC.

3. As a de facto sovereign, independent state, the ROC has a right to have official relations with any state and to become a member of intergovernmental organizations. The PRC has never governed Taiwan and cannot represent the people of Taiwan in the United Nations or other international organizations.

4. The temporary presence of two Chinese governments in the United Nations, like the presence of the two Germanys or the two Koreas, will facilitate, not obstruct reunification.

5. The ROC favors expanding trade, investment, and travel with

mainland China but requires that it be indirect and applies other restrictions as necessary to protect Taiwan's security and prosperity.

6. Taiwan and mainland China should be reunified. Negotiations on reunification can be undertaken when the PRC:
   (a). becomes a democracy with a free enterprise economic system;
   (b). drops the threat to use force against Taiwan; and
   (c). stops interfering with the expansion of the ROC's international relations.

The Democratic Progressive Party (DPP) Position[3]

1. An independent Republic of Taiwan should be established. A decision to this effect should be reached by a plebiscite among all of Taiwan's citizens.
2. Taiwan should seek membership in the UN as a new state, not on the German pattern as one of two Chinese states pending reunification.
3. Taiwan should resolve differences with the PRC by government-to-government negotiations.

Quasi-Official Negotiations

When the United States shifted its diplomatic relations from Taipei to Beijing in 1979, PRC authorities made a number of conciliatory moves toward Taiwan. They halted bombardment of the offshore islands with propaganda shells and appealed for discussions between the government of the PRC and the Taiwan authorities on ending the military confrontation. They proposed the establishment of direct communication, travel, and shipping services across the strait. ROC authorities, however, flatly rejected PRC proposals, announcing that their stand would be: "No contacts, no negotiations, no compromise." Chiang Ching-kuo reminded the people of Taiwan that "peace talks" with the Chinese Communists had led to the loss of the mainland; refusal to talk with them would foil their plot to employ "peace talks" as a united front tactic to subjugate Taiwan.[4]

Although the Taipei authorities rejected negotiations with Beijing, they came under increasing pressure from the people of Taiwan to relax the prohibition on travel to mainland China. Finally, in October 1987, Chiang Ching-kuo authorized travel through a third territory to the mainland to visit relatives. Soon tens of thousands were making the trip, most of them via Hong Kong, and within a few years the ROC had relaxed restrictions further to allow indirect trade, investment, tourism, and other forms of interaction with mainland China.

With increased interaction came problems that were difficult to resolve for governments that could not speak to each other. Foremost was the problem of illegal immigration into Taiwan by thousands of persons from mainland China seeking a better life. In September 1990 the Red Cross societies of the two sides reached agreement on repatriating illegal immigrants and persons wanted for having committed crimes on one side or the other. In 1991 the two sides established quasi-official organizations authorized to negotiate with each other to resolve problems arising in people-to-people relations across the strait. These were the Straits Exchange Foundation (SEF) on the Taiwan side and the Association for Relations Across the Taiwan Strait (ARATS) in mainland China. These organizations dealt with practical problems only; they were not authorized to discuss political differences between the two sides.[5]

Even in seeking solutions to practical problems, however, political implications proved difficult to avoid. The PRC was determined not to imply recognition of Taiwan as a separate political entity, while the ROC was equally determined not to accept agreements implying that Taiwan was part of the PRC. Thus, negotiations on such seemingly simple matters as the authentication of legal documents or the handling of registered mail dragged on. Eventually, at a meeting in Singapore in April 1993 Koo Chen-fu and Wang Daohan, the chairmen of SEF and ARATS, signed agreements on these two matters and agreed on a schedule for future meetings of the two organizations.

Progress was made in subsequent negotiations regarding procedures for handling fishing disputes, the repatriation of illegal immigrants, and the return of hijackers, but final agreement had not been reached on these issues by May 28, 1995, when the vice chairmen of ARATS and SEF, Tang Shubei and Chiao Jen-ho, met in Taipei to work out the agenda for the second Koo-Wang meeting, scheduled for July 20 in Beijing. These talks reportedly went well, despite the U.S. announcement on May 22 that Lee Teng-hui would be allowed to visit Cornell. For the first time, ROC officials (two department heads from the Mainland Affairs Council) attended the SEF-ARATS talks in the capacity of expert advisers. A PRC news service reported that these talks had "made many breakthroughs in such areas as the channel, structure and content for cross-strait consultations."[6]

At a press conference in Taipei, Tang expressed satisfaction with the results of the consultations and said that he would return to Beijing and make further preparations for the second Wang-Koo meeting. He also said: "ARATS and SEF now operate when the two sides have political differences. ARATS always maintains that the two sides' political differences should not affect the two associations' operations." When Tang returned to Beijing, he was congratulated by Chen Yunlin, deputy executive director of the State Council's Taiwan Affairs Office, who said: "The achievements in the preliminary consultations show that despite both sides' differences in politics, extensive common ground still remains in the development of cross-strait relations."[7]

Sometime during the next two weeks, PRC leaders decided that the SEF-ARATS channel could not remain unaffected by adverse political developments. Perhaps they were persuaded by the contents of Lee's Cornell speech and the almost simultaneous appearance of ROC Premier Lien Chan in Europe. In any case, on June 16 ARATS officials wrote to SEF, postponing the Koo-Wang meeting "because the Taiwan side has taken a series of actions to undermine relations between the two sides of the Taiwan Strait, which has seriously affected the talks." One of the PRC's mouthpieces in Hong Kong, the *Wen Wei Po*, declared that Lee's activities in the United States had "poisoned relations across the strait. . . . If Beijing did not take measures to stop him and did not put off the Wang-Koo talks and pertinent consultations, it virtually would have meant conniving at and tolerating the adverse current of splitting the country which has emerged in Taiwan."[8]

Thus, although the SEF-ARATS channel remained open for the exchange of messages, the regularly scheduled meetings between officials of these organizations at various levels, at which slow but encouraging progress had been made toward institutionalizing the management of the complex relations between the two sides, were suspended.

Efforts to Revive the SEF-ARATS Talks

ROC spokesmen expressed disappointment at the PRC's decision to suspend the SEF-ARATS talks. The official body responsible for policy toward the PRC, the Mainland Affairs Council (MAC), said that political problems should not affect talks between these two unofficial bodies that had been established to resolve functional problems arising out of cross-strait exchanges. The statement reiterated the ROC's determination to pursue national reunification and denied that the ROC was trying to create "two Chinas" or "one China, one Taiwan." The MAC added, however, that in order to sustain its own existence, the ROC must broaden the scope of its participation in the world community.[9]

In August 1995 ARAT's chairman, Wang Daohan, told a visiting delegation from Taiwan that until Taiwan took the initiative to clarify its stand on the "one China principle" and the "sovereignty issue," technical talks between ARATS and SEF and a Wang-Koo meeting could not be held. He said that the PRC was very firm on this issue and would never make a concession.[10]

Senior Taiwan spokespeople frequently urged the resumption of the SEF-ARATS talks, pointing out that these would provide an appropriate channel through which to make the necessary arrangements for the meetings of top leaders proposed by Jiang Zemin. In April 1996 Wang Daohan issued a statement blaming Taiwan for having "sabotaged" the basis for negotiations betweeen ARATS and SEF. He said that if Taiwan really wanted a second Wang-Koo meeting, it should stop its activities of creating "two Chinas" or "one China, one Taiwan" and return to the one China principle with concrete action.[11]

Koo Chen-fu, SEF's chairman, denied that his side had transgressed the one China principle. He said that both sides were engaged in a process of seeking unification, after which China naturally would be one. At the present time, Koo said, the two sides needed "to return to the process of seeking unification."[12] SEF sent a letter to ARATS proposing the reopening of talks, but ARATS rejected the proposal, again demanding that Taiwan "return to the one China principle by concrete action."

In response to queries as to what the PRC meant by "returning to the one China principle by concrete action," Tang Shubei and other PRC spokespeople indicated that Taiwan should: (a) abandon its campaign to join the United Nations, (b) stop seeking dual recognition, and (c) stop sending its leaders on visits to countries that have diplomatic relations with the PRC. Tang said that practical steps toward opening direct communication, trade, and travel between Taiwan and mainland China would also help to improve cross-strait relations.[13] Another Beijing spokesman added a fourth condition: that Taiwan must stop making large purchases of advanced foreign weapons.[14]

By January 1997 many in Taiwan had concluded that the PRC had deliberately laid down conditions for the resumption of SEF-ARATS talks that it knew to be unacceptable to the Taiwan authorities in order to further postpone the resumption of the talks. The prevailing view in Taiwan was that Jiang Zemin was too deeply involved in managing the Hong Kong transition in June–July 1997 and preparing for the 15th Party Congress in the fall of the year to be able to take on at this time the delicate task of negotiating with Taiwan.

During the months following the suspension of the SEF-ARATS talks, it became evident that the talks could not be resumed without a political understanding between the two sides on the issue of the one China principle. The PRC was no longer willing to adhere to the agreement reached in November 1992 that both sides would express their commitment to the one China principle but each would define it in its own way, allowing talks on practical problems to proceed. Now, the PRC insisted, political differences had to be addressed. Over this period the ROC edged toward a willingness to open political negotiations with the PRC, primarily through an exchange of public statements by Lee Teng-hui and Jiang Zemin.

Arms-Length, Top-Level Negotiations

Before Lee's Cornell visit, an attempt to break the political impasse had been made by Jiang Zemin, general secretary of the CCP, with an important speech on January 30, 1995.[15] Jiang reiterated the PRC's basic position, stated earlier. "We consistently stand for achieving reunification by peaceful means and through negotiations," he declared. "But we shall not undertake not to use force. Such a commitment would only make it impossible to achieve peaceful unification and could not but lead to the eventual settlement of the question by the use of force."

Jiang encapsulated the PRC's position in eight numbered paragraphs that subsequently became known as "Jiang's eight points." He repeated an earlier statement: "On the premise that there is only one China, we are prepared to talk with the Taiwan authorities about any matter, including the form that official meetings should take." He then made a proposal that PRC officials and scholars pointed to as a new departure: "I suggest that, as the first step, negotiations should be held and an agreement reached on officially ending the state of hostility between the two sides in accordance with the principle that there is only one China" (Point 3).

Jiang urged making great efforts to expand cross-strait economic exchanges and cooperation and to speed up the establishment of direct postal, air, and shipping services. He promised to safeguard the legitimate rights and interests of Taiwan businesspeople and recommended signing nongovernmental agreements for the protection of these rights and interests. He declared that "political differences should not affect or interfere with the economic cooperation between the two sides" (Point 5).

Jiang referred to "the splendid culture of the Chinese nation" as "an important basis for the reunification of the motherland" and urged people on both sides of the strait to "carry forward the fine traditions of Chinese culture" (Point 6).

Finally, Jiang welcomed visits to the mainland by "leaders of the Taiwan authorities . . . in appropriate capacities." He added: "We are also ready to accept invitations from the Taiwan side to visit Taiwan. We can discuss state affairs or exchange ideas on certain questions first. Even a simple visit to the other side will be useful" (Point 8).

Taipei cautiously welcomed Jiang's speech. Lee Teng-hui referred to it as a "very important" development and said that it should be carefully studied.[16] In comments to the Legislative Yuan on February 21, Premier Lien Chan agreed with Jiang on the importance of increasing economic exchange but called on the PRC to treat Taiwan as a political entity and to respect its right to international survival.[17] Foreign Minister Frederick Chien denounced the PRC for its rigidity in restricting Taiwan's international maneuvering room.[18]

On April 8 Lee Teng-hui gave an authoritative six-point response to Jiang's eight points.[19] Two of his points paralleled Jiang's: increasing bilateral exchanges based on Chinese culture (Lee's Point 2) and enhancing economic relations. With respect to the latter, Lee declared that "Taiwan should make the mainland its economic hinterland, while the mainland should use Taiwan as a model of development" (Lee's Point 3).

Several other points took sharp issue with Jiang. Lee called for unification based on the reality that the two sides are governed by two governments, neither subordinate to the other (Lee's Point 1). Lee urged that both sides join international organizations on an equal footing. Repeating a proposal he had made previously, Lee suggested that both sides could meet in a natural manner on international occasions (Lee's Point 4). Jiang had already rejected this idea, saying that "the affairs of the Chinese people should be handled by ourselves, something that does not take an international occasion to accomplish" (Jiang's Point 8).

Responding to Jiang's recommendation for negotiations to end the state of hostility between the two sides, Lee pointed out that in 1991 he had renounced the use of force against the mainland and he now called for a similar public renunciation of force against Taiwan, "thus paving the way for formal negotiations between both sides to put an end to the state of hostility" (Lee's Point 5).

Finally, Lee proposed that the two sides "jointly safeguard prosperity and promote democracy in Hong Kong and Macau" (Lee's Point 6).

PRC commentators expressed disappointment at Lee's response to Jiang's "eight points."[20] They found little new in his statement. Instead of responding to Jiang's proposal to negotiate an end to the state of hostilities, Lee demanded that the PRC first renounce the use of force. Instead of accepting an exchange of visits by leaders of the two sides, Lee continued to insist that leaders see each other on international occasions. Lee's stress on Taiwan as a separate political entity, entitled to join international organizations on an equal footing with the PRC, appeared to commentators to demonstrate Lee's commitment to create two Chinas. While focusing on the foregoing criticisms of Lee's statements, mainland commentators disregarded those parts of the statement that reiterated the ROC's goal of national reunification.

Before the two sides had adequate time in which to consider the next step in their arms-length negotiations through public statements by the two leaders, Lee's visit to Cornell in June 1995 brought the process to an abrupt halt. Ever since the collapse of the Soviet Union eliminated the principal strategic rationale for U.S.-PRC cooperation, Beijing authorities had watched with concern actions by the United States and Taiwan that seemed to them to be moving Taiwan away from unification and toward independence. These actions included the sale of F-16s to Taiwan in 1992, the initiation of the ROC's UN campaign in 1993, the upgrading of contacts with Taipei by the Clinton administration's Taiwan policy review in 1994, Lee Teng-hui's "private" visits to Southeast Asia and the Middle East in 1994 and 1995 and Premier Lien Chan's trip to Austria, Hungary, and the Czech Republic in June 1995. Thus, Lee's Cornell visit was seen, not as a single unfriendly act about which Chinese leaders had been lied to by American spokesmen, but as the apogee of a series of pro-independence actions. PRC authorities decided that the time had come to draw a line in the sand.

While PRC officials waited uneasily for the presidential election in Taiwan to take place and prepared the military exercises for March 1996, they issued another authoritative statement on PRC-Taiwan relations. This time Premier Li Peng, on the first anniversary of Jiang Zemin's January 30, 1995, speech, called attention to the importance of the PRC statement. Li stressed that it contained the essence of Deng Xiaoping's thought on "peaceful reunification" and "one country, two systems." Li confirmed the continuing validity of Jiang's "eight points."

Li condemned "the arch-criminal" who promoted Taiwan independence and undermined China's reunification and said that since June the previous year, the Chinese people had waged a struggle against "Taiwan independence," a struggle that "will not cease even for a single day, so long as the Taiwan authorities' activities to split the motherland continue." Alluding to the forthcoming election, Li warned that "no matter how the ways of producing a leader on Taiwan may change, the fact that Taiwan is a part of China's territory will not change and the fact that the leader in Taiwan is only the leader of a region in China will not change."[21]

Li's reiteration of Jiang's "eight points" made no change in the PRC's basic Taiwan policy. It did, however, reaffirm that Jiang's proposals for reciprocal visits by leaders of the two sides and for negotiations on ending the state of hostilities remained valid. There had been speculation that Jiang's relatively moderate proposals had been super-seded by the hard line taken after the Cornell visit. Unconfirmed Hong Kong press reports alleged that Jiang had lost face and come under criticism from military hard-liners for being too conciliatory toward Taiwan and for having been misled by the United States. Li's speech, however, made clear that Jiang's formulation continued to be official policy. Now PRC leaders would wait for the results of the election to see how Lee would respond.

During the election campaign, Lee had promised to give priority to cross-strait relations after the election. On May 20, in his inaugural ad-dress, Lee called on governments on both sides of the strait

> to deal straightforwardly with the momentous question of how to termi-nate the state of hostility between them, which will make a crucial contri-bution to the historic tasks of unification. In the future, at the call of my country and with the support of its people, I would like to embark on a journey of peace to mainland China, taking with me the consensus and will of the 21.3 million people. I am also ready to meet with the top lead-ership of the Chinese Communists for a direct exchange of views in order to open up a new era of communication and cooperation between the two sides and ensure peace, stability and prosperity in the Asia-Pacific region.

Thus, Lee responded to Jiang's "eight points" more positively than he had in his April 1995 "six points." In calling for efforts to end the state of hostility between the two sides, he dropped the precondition of a PRC renunciation of force, and in offering to meet with PRC leaders he no longer insisted on doing so on an international occasion. He said he would make his "journey of peace" to mainland China with "the consensus and will" of the people of Taiwan. Such a consensus was to be sought at a national development conference.

Lee ruled out Taiwan independence as "totally unnecessary and im-possible," but he pointed out that for forty years the two sides of the strait had been two separate jurisdictions. He said that although "both sides pursue eventual national unification, only when both sides face up to the facts and engage in dialogue with profound sincerity and pa-tience will they be able to find the solution to the unification ques-tion."[22]

From the PRC's viewpoint, the positive aspects of Lee's address were overshadowed by his statement that "the ROC has always been a sovereign state" and his determination to "continue to promote prag-matic diplomacy" in order to "secure for our 21.3 million people enough room for existence and development as well as the respect and treatment they deserve in the international arena."

PRC leaders may also have found demeaning Lee's statement that "equipped with a much higher level of education and development than in other parts of China, Taiwan is set to gradually exercise its leadership role in cultural development and take upon itself the responsibility for nurturing a new Chinese culture." Lee also offered Taiwan's developmental experience "as an aid in mapping the direction of development in mainland China."

PRC commentators were highly critical of Lee's address, condemning in particular his claim of ROC sovereignty, his adherence to pragmatic diplomacy, and his failure to commit himself unmistakably to the one-China principle.[23] Commentators glossed over or explained away Lee's rejection of Taiwan independence and his offer to travel to the mainland to negotiate an end to the state of hostilities.

Direct Trade and Travel

From 1979 onward, the PRC pressed vigorously for the Taiwan authorities to permit direct trade and travel between Taiwan and mainland China. As Taiwan's economic relations with the mainland increased, growing numbers of businesspeople in Taiwan urged the government to permit direct trade and travel in order to save them the added expense of having to conduct business through Hong Kong. The Taiwan authorities, however, declined to modify their policy of requiring indirect trade and travel, on the grounds that allowing ships and planes to go directly between Taiwan and the mainland would increase the security risk to Taiwan.

Not all officials in Taipei, however, agreed with the indirect shipment requirement. As early as December 1993, Economics Minister P. K. Chiang publicly advocated establishing direct shipping links between Taiwan and mainland ports on the grounds that it would reduce transportation costs and make Taiwan industries more competitive. The minister of transportation and communication supported Chiang's proposal, but the vice chairman of the Mainland Affairs Council and the chairman of the Council for Economic Planning and Development both said that his proposal was premature.[24]

During the period from 1990 to 1996, airline and shipping company executives on various occasions traveled to mainland China and Taiwan to discuss with their counterparts how to conduct direct cross-strait trade and travel, once it had been authorized by the government in Taipei. They held seminars in Beijing, Shanghai, and Taipei on direct trade and travel and inspected port and airport facilities on both sides of the strait. For example, in July 1996 a delegation of port directors from nine of the China mainland's principal ports spent nine days visiting four ports in Taiwan to discuss technical questions involved in direct trade and travel.

The Taipei authorities continued to resist pressures from Taiwan companies to approve direct cross-strait trade and travel, often repeating the formula that the PRC must first recognize Taiwan as a political entity, renounce the use of force and stop interfering with Taiwan's international activities.[25] Pressures increased, however, particularly after the decision was announced in January 1995 to make Taiwan an Asian-Pacific Regional Operations Center for transnational corporations. Skeptics doubted that many companies would choose to establish their regional headquarters in Taiwan unless they had direct access by sea and air to the economy of mainland China.

Another form of pressure on the Taiwan authorities to authorize direct shipping was the growing tendency of Taiwan businesspeople to falsify manifests, showing shipment via Hong Kong when the shipment actually went direct to a mainland port.[26] Shipments were difficult to police and failure to address this issue, to bring law in line with practice, would lead to increasing disrespect for the law.

In December 1994 Taipei came up with a proposal that was widely regarded as a first step toward direct cross-strait shipping. The proposal was to establish in Kaohsiung an "offshore transshipment center" where goods could be offloaded and transferred to ships sailing direct to mainland ports. Only ships registered in foreign countries would be permitted to make the direct trip to and from the mainland. The cargo would originate in, or be destined for, third countries; it would not pass through Taiwan customs into or out of Taiwan. These direct routes were designated as neither domestic nor international but "special routes."[27]

The PRC criticized this proposal as not constituting direct cross-strait shipping. In August 1996 it made a counterproposal, issuing regulations for direct passenger and cargo shipping from Xiamen and Fuzhou to Taiwan ports. Designated as "domestic routes under special management," these routes would be limited to ships registered in mainland China or Taiwan.[28] This PRC announcement came only a few days after two of Taiwan's leading businesspeople, Chang Yung-fa, chairman of the Evergreen Group, and Wang Yung-ching, chairman of the Formosa Plastics Group, appealed publicly for the Taipei government to approve the establishment of direct shipping links.[29]

In January 1997 shipping associations from mainland China and Taiwan meeting in Hong Kong announced that they had reached a consensus on cross-strait shipping. Shipments between Kaohsiung's transshipment center and Xiamen began in April 1997. The 5,000-ton *Sheng*

Da, a mainland-owned ship registered in St. Vincent, docked in Kaohsiung on April 20 with 30 containers, a fraction of its 250-container capacity. On April 25 the first Taiwan-owned ship, the *Uni Order*, registered in Panama, docked in Xiamen. By July, 146 trips had been made between Fujian and Kaohsiung, transporting 36,000 containers.[30]

Ships traversing this route were often less than half full, but PRC companies reportedly had orders to maintain a regular schedule, regardless of the availability of cargo. The two governments had approved five government-owned mainland companies and six private Taiwan companies to operate the cross-strait routes. Although the transshipment cost per container was considerably less than the cost of transshipment via Hong Kong, shippers were slow to take advantage of the new center, and Taiwan shipping companies complained that they were losing money because of the small size of the cargoes. Nevertheless, they continued to ply the routes in the hope that the PRC would soon open Shanghai and other large ports to cross-strait shipping. Xiamen had an annual capacity of 330,000 TEUs (twenty-foot equivalent container units) and Fuzhou only 150,000, compared to Kaohsiung's annual capacity of 5 million.[31]

Both governments had made concessions in order to initiate this limited form of cross-strait shipping. The PRC agreed to the ROC's requirement that the ships be foreign-registered, and Taiwan dropped its ban on mainland-owned ships entering Taiwan harbors. Beijing undoubtedly hoped that the transshipment center would be the first step toward true direct cross-strait shipping and may have withheld the big port of Shanghai in part as a bargaining chip. Beijing may also have felt that allowing Kaohsiung to become a transshipment point for goods going to and from Shanghai might reduce Hong Kong's role as a transshipment center just at the time that it was making a critical adjustment to its new status as a special administrative region of the PRC.

In early 1998 the two sides agreed on another step to facilitate cross-strait shipping. The Taipei-based Taiwan Strait Shipping Association met in Bangkok with the Beijing-based Strait Shipping Exchange Association in February 1998, accompanied by transportation officials of the two governments acting as advisers, to discuss ways of improving cross-strait shipping. As a result of this meeting, the ROC Ministry of Transportation and Communication announced that cargo ships would be permitted to travel between Shanghai and Keelung, with a brief stop at the Japanese island of Ishigaki, about 150 miles east of Keelung. The Shanghai-Ishigaki-Keelung route, by opening Shanghai to nearly direct shipping, should provide significant savings for traders.[32]

Discussions on direct flights from Taiwan to mainland China were less advanced than the negotiations on direct shipping, but Taipei approved several steps that facilitated travel to the China mainland via Hong Kong and Macau. In October 1995 Taipei reached agreement with Air Macau that its aircraft could carry passengers from Taipei to Macau's newly opened international airport, pause there for half an hour, then, with a change in flight number, carry them on to a mainland China airport. Air Macau is 51 percent owned by China National Aviation Corporation, a wholly owned subsidiary of the PRC's Civil Aviation Administration of China.[33]

In June 1996 Taiwan and Hong Kong airlines reached a five-year agreement, approved by the ROC government and by the Chinese-British Joint Liaison Group on Hong Kong, for the continuation of aviation services between Taiwan and Hong Kong. China Airlines and Eva Airlines in Taiwan and Cathay Pacific and Dragonair in Hong Kong were designated to provide the service. In order to reach agreement, the Taiwan side had to replace the China Airlines tail logo of the national flag with a plum blossom and permit Dragonair, which was 64 percent owned by the PRC's China National Aviation Corporation and China International Trust and Investment Corporation, to fly to Taiwan. Dragonair, like Macau Air, is allowed to fly Taiwan passengers to mainland airports after a brief stop and a change of flight numbers in Hong Kong.[34]

The PRC and the ROC have handled the issue of direct trade and travel with both economic and political objectives in mind. For the PRC, the establishment of direct trade and travel would link Taiwan more firmly to the mainland, promote the economic integration of the two areas, and reduce the risk that Taiwan authorities would declare the island a separate, independent state. For the ROC, the issue is more complex. Taiwan businesspeople with investments on the mainland, including influential business leaders, strongly favor the opening of direct links. The absence of direct links is also a significant impediment to the transformation of Taiwan into an Asian-Pacific Regional Operations Center, which the Taipei government considers crucial to the future position of the island in the world economy. On the other hand, the PRC has shown little inclination to make the political concessions that are frequently demanded by ROC officials as conditions for authorizing direct links. Security officials also have serious concerns regarding the increased risk to Taiwan's security that direct links would create. And the DPP opposes direct links unless they are defined as international routes, a position that neither the PRC nor the ROC accepts.

In October 1997 business circles increased their pressure on the government to establish direct links. Returning from a visit to Beijing, Chang Yung-fa, chairman of the Evergreen Group, publicly declared that the time was ripe for negotiations with the PRC and urged the government to promptly establish direct links. He said that these could no longer be regarded as bargaining chips in negotiations with the PRC and that failure to establish them would cause a decline in the competitiveness of Taiwan firms. Other leading businesspeople spoke up in support of Chang's views, although several would hold back on establishing directs links until the SEF-ARATS formal talks had been resumed.[35]

With the SEF-ARATS channel in suspension, the direct links issue was the only area in which talks between the two sides took place through unofficial channels, supervised by the two governments. Airlines and shipping associations served as surrogate government representatives. By the end of 1997 agreement had been reached on Taiwan–Hong Kong flights, but no serious negotiations had taken place on direct Taiwan-mainland flights. Limited direct shipping had begun between Xiamen, Fuzhou, and Kaohsiung, and arrangements for the continuation of Hong Kong–Taiwan shipping had been set in place, as will be discussed further on.

In early 1996 the PRC took initiatives in respect to the third of the "three links," direct communication. The minister of posts and telecommunication proposed direct exchange of mail across the strait and the laying of a cross-strait fiber-optic cable between Taiwan and the mainland.[36] The director-general of telecommunications also proposed laying a fiber-optic cable across the strait, pointing out that the use of indirect telecommunications links cost Taiwan and the PRC some $20 million each in fees to third parties.[37] In a meeting with Lee Teng-hui in April 1996, I pointed out that South Korea and the PRC had recently opened a fiber-optic cable and suggested that a similar cable across the Taiwan Strait would not only save money, but would be the least risky way to create a symbolic link between Taiwan and mainland China. Lee's response was that indirect telecommunication didn't cost much.

While the ROC did not accept these PRC proposals, it did authorize the state-run Chunghwa Telecom to invest, along with the PRC and other countries, in two cable networks that by the end of 1999 would have terminals in mainland China and Taiwan, enabling these two places to communicate with each other, as well as with the United States and a number of Asian and European countries.[38]

Taiwan–Hong Kong Relations

The transfer of Hong Kong to the PRC on July 1, 1997, forced the ROC to rethink its relationship with Hong Kong and with the PRC. Hong

Kong became a "special administrative region" (SAR) of the PRC, with different political and economic systems from those of the mainland. The PRC envisaged a similar status for Taiwan after reunification but with a greater degree of autonomy. The ROC, however, rejected the idea that Hong Kong under the "one country, two systems" concept would be a model for Taiwan's future relations with the PRC.

Taiwan has an extraordinarily close economic relationship with Hong Kong. Most of the trade and investment by Taiwan businesspeople in the China mainland has been conducted through Hong Kong. In 1995 two-way trade between Taiwan and Hong Kong was $28.1 billion, Taiwan investment in Hong Kong exceeded $4 billion, and more than three thousand Taiwan firms had registered to do business in Hong Kong.[39] How would these activities be managed when Hong Kong was part of the PRC?

In June 1995 PRC Vice Premier Qian Qichen announced seven principles to govern Hong Kong–Taiwan relations, which he characterized as "a special component of the relations between the two sides of the Taiwan Strait." Qian said that people-to-people relations between Hong Kong and Taiwan would remain basically unchanged, as long as people from Taiwan obeyed Hong Kong's Basic Law and did nothing to violate the one China principle or to damage Hong Kong's stability and prosperity. Taiwan's existing organizations and personnel in Hong Kong could remain, as long as they did nothing inconsistent with their registered character. Shipping and air traffic between Hong Kong and Taiwan would be managed as "special regional lines." Official contacts and agreements between the Hong Kong SAR and the Taiwan region had to be approved by the central government of the PRC.[40]

The government of the ROC declared that it intended to maintain economic, cultural, educational, and other ties with Hong Kong after July 1, 1997. It would regard Hong Kong and Macau as "special regions," different from other areas of the mainland, and its relations with those territories would be governed by a Statute on Relations with Hong Kong and Macau. This statute, which was adopted by the Legislative Yuan in March 1997, envisaged little change in sea and air transportation between Hong Kong and Taiwan after the changeover but recognized that PRC approval would be required.

The ROC stated its intention of retaining its governmental agencies in Hong Kong. These included the Chung Hwa Travel Service, which represented Taiwan's Foreign Ministry and issued entry permits for Taiwan, and the Kwang Hwa Information and Cultural Center, representing the Government Information Office. Since Hong Kong was no longer regarded as foreign territory after the changeover, the ROC transferred the management of the Chung Hwa Travel Service from the

Foreign Ministry to a newly established Hong Kong Affairs Bureau within the Mainland Affairs Council.

Shipping between Taiwan and Hong Kong continued without interruption after July 1, 1997, on the basis of an agreement reached on May 25 between a delegation headed by the deputy secretary-general of the SEF and the head of the Hong Kong Shipowners Association, which had been authorized by ARATS to negotiate on behalf of the Hong Kong SAR. Hong Kong–registered ships entering Taiwan harbors flew the SAR flag, which featured a bauhinia flower, on the aft mast and were not required, temporarily, to raise the ROC flag on the mainmast. Taiwan-registered ships entering Hong Kong harbor were permitted, temporarily, to fly no flag on either mast. Thus, the political implications of flag flying were avoided. It was not clear how long this "temporary" arrangement was intended to last.[41]

Koo Chen-fu, the chairman of the SEF, was invited to the handover ceremony in Hong Kong on July 1. On July 3 he had a cordial meeting with the chief executive of the Hong Kong SAR, at which the two men agreed that Hong Kong and Taiwan should establish institutionalized dialogue channels and expand exchanges in various fields. Tung instructed his special adviser, Paul Yip, to maintain regular contact with Taiwan's chief representative in Hong Kong. MAC vice chairman, Kao Koong-lian, said that Taiwan would welcome the establishment of a representative office of the Hong Kong SAR in Taipei.[42]

The governments on both sides of the Taiwan Strait have clearly indicated their desire for the interaction between Taiwan and Hong Kong to go forward much as it has in the past. Hong Kong will continue to provide crucial services to both parties as a kind of middle ground. Even if direct travel and shipping between Taiwan and the mainland should begin, many of Hong Kong's services and facilities would still be indispensable, especially to the large number of Taiwan investors in South China and in Hong Kong itself.

Notes

1. State Council, Taiwan Affairs Office and Information Office, *The Taiwan Question and the Reunification of China* (Beijing, August 1993).

2. Mainland Affairs Council, Taipei, "Explanation of Relations Across the Taiwan Strait," July 5, 1994 (in *FBIS*, [July 11, 1994]: 50–59).

3. *Democratic Progressive Party Charter and Program* (Taipei: August 1, 1995.)

4. Ralph N. Clough, *Reaching Across the Taiwan Strait* (Boulder, CO: Westview Press, 1993) p. 14.

5. Clough, *Reaching*, pp. 134–139.

6. Hong Kong *Zhongquo Tongxun She*, May 28, 1995 (in *FBIS* [June 12, 1995]: 73).

7. *Xinhua*, May 29, 1995 (in *FBIS* [May 30, 1995]: 82–83).

8. *Wen Hui Bao*, June 17, 1995 (in *FBIS* [June 21, 1995]: 95).

9. *Free China Journal* (June 23, 1995).

10. *Lien Ho Pao*, Aug. 29, 1995 (in *FBIS* [September 5, 1995]: 90–91).

11. *China Post* (April 30, 1996).

12. SEF, *Chiao Liu*, no. 27 (May 1996): 8.

13. *Renmin Ribao Overseas Edition*, October 9, 1996 (in *FBIS* [October 9, 1996]).

14. *Ta Kung Pao*, December 8, 1996, (quoted in *China Post* [December 9, 1996]).

15. *Xinhua*, January 30, 1995 (in *FBIS* [January 30, 1995]: 84–86. See Annex 1.

16. *China Post* (February 4, 1995).

17. *China Post* (February 22, 1995).

18. *Free China Journal* (March 10, 1995).

19. *China Post* (April 11, 1995). See Annex 2.

20. See, for example, comments by Chinese People's Consultative Conference member Xu Simin, Hong Kong, *Zhongguo Tongxun*, April 10, 1995 (in *FBIS* [April 18, 1995]: 95); and Beijing Central People's Radio broadcast to Taiwan, April 18, 1995 (in *FBIS* [April 20, l995]: 88–89).

21. *Xinhua*, (February l, 1996 via World News Connection [FBIS]).

22. Text of Lee's inaugural address in *China Post* (May 20, 1996).

23. See, for example, Hong Kong, *Zhongguo Tongxun She*, May 22, 1996 (*FBIS* [May 23, 1996]: 43–44); Hong Kong, *Wen Wei Po*, May 23, 1996 (*FBIS* [May 23, 1996]: 44–45); Hong Kong, *Sing Tao Jih Pao*, May 22, 1996 (*FBIS* [May 22, 1996]: 82).

24. *China Post* (December 30, 1993).

25. See, for example, the statement by the vice minister of the Ministry of Communication and Transportation, *China Post* (October 29, 1994).

26. Allen Y. Tso, "Calculating Cross-Strait Trade" *Issues and Studies*, vol. 32, no. 6, (June 1996): 53.

27. *Free China Journal* (December 23, 1994).

28. *Beijing Review*, (September 16–22, 1996): 9.

29. *China Post* (August 17, 1996).

30. *Xinhua* (October 7, 1997 via World News Connection [FBIS]).

31. Estimates supplied by the American Institute in Taiwan.

32. *Free China Journal* (March 6, 1998).

33. *Free China Journal* (October 20, 1995).

34. *Free China Journal* (June 22, 1996); *Chiao Liu*, no. 28, (July 1996): 75.

35. *China Times* (October 15,16,1997); *Far Eastern Economic Review*, November 6, 1997): 22, 26.

36. Beijing: Central People's Radio, February 12, 1996 (in *FBIS* [February 13, 1996]: 70).

37. Beijing: Central People's Radio, February 16, 1996 (in *FBIS* [February 20, 1996]: 62).

38. *China Post* (November 28, 1997).

39. Mainland Affairs Council, Taipei, *The Republic of China's Policy Toward Hong Kong and Macao* (May 1996) p. 11.

40. Beijing, *Xinhua*, June 22, 1995 (in *FBIS* [June 22, 1995]: 86).

41. *China Post* (May 26, 1997).

42. *Free China Journal* (July 7, 1997); *Chiao Liu*, no. 34, (August 1997): 6–8.

Chapter 4

People-to-People Activities

Although the governments in Beijing and Taipei made little progress in resolving the political impasse that developed after Lee Teng-hui's Cornell visit, relations between people on the two sides of the Taiwan Strait continued to flourish. Large numbers of businesspeople, academics, tourists, athletes, and others from Taiwan traveled across the strait, averaging over 1,000,000 visits per year. By 1997 visits to the mainland totaled more than 11,000,000 and visits to Taiwan 220,000.[1] In 1996 alone more than 55,000 visits took place from the mainland to Taiwan—about 40,000 visits to relatives, 5,000 for educational and cultural exchange programs, and 1,100 for trade.

Opportunities for investment and trade in the immense, rapidly growing economy on the China mainland presented an irresistible attraction to entrepreneurs in Taiwan. The two economies were complementary. The mainland offered natural resources, less expensive land than Taiwan, a huge market, and an inexhaustible supply of cheap labor. Taiwan provided capital, technology, and managerial and marketing skills. Knowledge of the Chinese language and customs gave Taiwan investors a distinct advantage over investors from other countries. By 1995 some 30,000 firms in Taiwan had invested an estimated $20 to $30 billion in the mainland.[2] Two-way trade in 1996 amounted to $23.8 billion.[3] Taiwan's exports to the China mainland and Hong Kong combined were only slightly less than exports to the United States, Taiwan's principal market.

Many visits to the China mainland were for other than business reasons. China's scenic and historic sites attracted tens of thousands of tourists from Taiwan. Specialists in a wide variety of fields exchanged delegations and conducted seminars. Performing arts troupes presented shows on the other side of the strait. Taiwanese seeking family roots visited ancestral villages in Fujian or Guangdong. Institutions with common interests developed regular exchanges. Believers in folk religions visited sacred sites. Athletes competed in meets on the other side of the strait.

The variety and intensity of the interchanges demonstrated the affinities of language, history, and culture that draw the two sides of the strait together. Clearly, people in Taiwan and mainland China have much in common. Whether the forces drawing them together will be sufficient to overcome their political differences remains to be seen.

Economic Integration

The trend toward economic integration between Taiwan and mainland China was driven primarily by the opportunities for profit-making that were perceived by individuals. Taiwan investors took the initiative, setting up wholly owned or joint-venture enterprises on the mainland.

At first, investors behaved cautiously, making small investments in the nearby provinces of Fujian or Guangdong, looking to recover their capital within two or three years. Gradually, larger firms began to participate, making larger, longer-term investments and the investment targets moved northward, to Shanghai, Jiangsu, and north China. Many of the firms manufacturing labor-intensive products for export simply moved all or part of their production from Taiwan to the mainland and continued exporting from there, but when it became possible to sell on the mainland market, the attraction of operating in the PRC was greatly enhanced. By 1995 37 percent of Taiwan's large, "blue chip" companies had invested in the mainland and 54 percent did business there.[4]

Taiwan's largest food manufacturer, President Enterprises Group, began investing in the mainland in 1991 and by May 1995 had invested $150 million in eighteen plants. President's chairman, Kao Ching-yuan, told the press that his company planned to build three or four factories a year, aiming at having at least one in each province, with a total investment exceeding $1 billion in ten years.[5] Disturbed by the PRC's military exercises in July and August 1995, Kao, who was also chairman of the China National Federation of Industries and a member of the KMT's central standing committee, called on Taiwan firms to halt their investments for the time being and said that his company would restudy its plans for the future.[6]

By February 1996, however, Kao was in Helongjiang province, surveying investment possibilities and the press reported that President was investing $1.53 million in a pharmaceutical plant in Suzhou and $6 million in an animal feed factory in Guangdong.[7] By mid-1996 President's cumulative investment had reached $300 million.[8] In August

1996 Kao led a group of sixty senior executives to a conference in Beijing, where Jiang Zemin told them that political differences should not be allowed to interfere with economic cooperation between the two sides of the strait. Jiang pledged to continue to encourage Taiwan investors and to protect their legitimate rights.[9]

In September 1996 President abandoned a plan to invest $100 million in two power plants in Wuhan, mainly because of a failure to agree on terms with its mainland partners but also in accord with Lee Teng-hui's appeal in the National Assembly in August to slow down mainland investment.[10] Other President projects on the mainland went forward. In December 1996 the company announced that it planned to open a discount store in Tianjin in 1997 together with the French Carrefours Group, with whom it operated ten large stores in Taiwan.[11] President Enterprises Group moved its investment holding company from Hong Kong to Shanghai to better supervise mainland operations. President executives stated that, although mainland operations would incur a loss of about $4 million in 1997, they were confident that revenues and profits from mainland operations would eventually surpass those from its business in Taiwan.[12]

Another Taiwan foodstuff company, the Ting Hsin Group, entered the mainland market in 1992 through its subsidiary, Tingyi Holdings, registered in the Cayman Islands, but operating only in China. Its Master Kang–brand instant noodles have been a great success. In early 1996 the 17 million packets and bowls per day produced by Tingyi factories in four cities and distributed through a nationwide sales network held 23.5 percent of the instant noodle market. Tingyi had no trouble raising $180 million in Hong Kong to finance further expansion; its stock issue was oversubscribed fifteen times.[13] By October 1997 the Ting Hsin Group's total investment on the mainland reached $1 billion, making it Taiwan's largest mainland investor.[14] In May 1998, Ting Hsin, which is vying with President to become the largest food distributor among the world's Chinese population, took over Wei Chuan, Taiwan's second largest food distributor, which also had extensive operations on the mainland.[15]

Food was the most basic commodity luring large Taiwan firms into the gigantic mainland market, but transportation was a close second. Taiwan's largest bicycle maker, Giant Manufacturing Co., investing through its Singapore holding company, built a plant in Qunshan, Jiangsu in 1994. By 1997 the plant's annual production was expected to reach one million bicycles, nearly half of Giant's worldwide production (one million from all plants in Taiwan and 100,000 from a newly built plant in Amsterdam.)[16]

The more prosperous regions of China were following Taiwan's path, advancing from a bicycle to a motorcycle economy. Consequently, Taiwan's leading motorcycle manufacturer, the Kwang Yang Motor Company (KYMCO), invested in four joint ventures on the mainland, that are expected to come on line in 1997 with an output of 50,000 to 100,000 units. Since the PRC requires motorcycle manufacturers to purchase 40 percent of their parts locally, thirty Taiwan firms associated with KYMCO established production bases on the mainland to supply parts. At a meeting in Guangzhou in late 1996 KYMCO's president, Wang Guangdong, announced plans to surpass Honda by 2010 as the world's largest name-brand motorcycle maker at a cost of some $1.5 billion. To reach this goal, KYMCO was not only expanding its operations in mainland China but also building new plants in Taiwan, Indonesia, India, Vietnam, and the Philippines.[17]

Automobile makers in Taiwan, restricted by Taiwan's small market, have also been sounding out possibilities on the mainland. China Motor Co., Taiwan's largest car manufacturer (16.5 percent owned by Japan's Mitsubishi Motor) has announced a $200 million plan to make vans in Fujian province in a joint venture with the Fujian Automobile Industry (Group) Corporation. Taiwan auto parts makers have also invested or plan to invest in mainland plants to supply China Motor or other mainland customers. Taiwan automobile manufacturers may find it more difficult than other Taiwan industries to break into the mainland market, however, for the PRC has tended to limit investments in the automobile industry to the world's largest companies and has insisted on cutting-edge technologies.

Taiwan's computer industry has begun shifting the manufacture of some of its products to the mainland. For example, Acer Corporation, Taiwan's largest computer conglomerate, has a keyboard plant in Guangzhou and another plant in Suzhou to make monitors and keyboards. Acer has also entered into a joint venture with the Legend Group, the largest PC maker in the PRC, to introduce Acer's new $500 basic computer.[18] According to press reports, Acer aims at becoming the largest computer manufacturer on the mainland and is shifting its distribution center from Hong Kong to Shenzhen. It is building a computer and motherboard plant in Guangdong and planned to construct two other factories in north China, for a total new investment of $10.9 million in 1997.[19] Another computer company in Taiwan, the GVC Corporation, joined with Japan's NEC and Packard-Bell to produce computer monitors in Guangzhou, and Logitech International, a Swiss company working through a Taiwan subsidiary, produces computer mice in a Suzhou plant.[20] Taiwan has become the world's third largest producer of information products (after the United States and Japan), and one-third of the Taiwan information industry's total output is produced in plants located in mainland China.[21]

The most striking example of reliance on mainland factories is in the production of computer casings. In 1997 Taiwan firms supplied 73 percent of the world market for this product, 70 percent of which was produced in mainland plants.[22]

The foregoing are but a few examples of the wide range of manufactured products being produced in the China mainland by Taiwan firms, including some of the largest industrial groups. The trend is toward larger investments, longer-term commitments, more advanced technology and plans to rely heavily on mainland production to achieve global ambitions.

A Slowdown in Trade and Investment

The military exercises during 1995 and 1996 adversely affected Taiwan's investment on the mainland and two-way trade. According to the PRC's Minister of Foreign Trade and Economic Cooperation, Wu Yi, between July and September 1995, contracted investment declined 28 percent and actually utilized investment declined 20 percent, compared to the same period of 1994. Two-way trade in this period increased only 1 percent, as compared to 21 percent in 1994.[23]

In 1996, according to Taiwan's Board of Foreign Trade, two-way trade increased only 5.8 percent to $22 billion, in comparison with double-digit growth in previous years.[24] Accurate figures on Taiwan's investment are more difficult to obtain. A mainland official source estimated that actual investment from Taiwan declined 10 percent during 1996,[25] but a Taiwan official source estimated the flow of Taiwan funds into the mainland at about the same level as 1995.[26]

The slowdown in Taiwan's trade and investment in mainland China during 1996 should not be attributed solely to the PRC's threatening political stance; a number of other factors also had an effect:

—gradual elimination of preferential treatment for Taiwan entrepreneurs;
—rising cost of land, labor, parts, and raw materials;
—trade disputes;
—difficulty in obtaining loans; and
—losses suffered by some investors.

Government Policies

The PRC government acted vigorously to counter the adverse effect on Taiwan investments of its threatening military moves. Not only did it send Tang Shubei to south China in the summer of 1995 to reassure Taiwan investors and warmly receive the Kao Ching-yuan mission as mentioned previously; later, in the fall of 1996 and the spring of 1997, it also sent several high-level economic officials, heading sizeable delegations, to Taiwan, including the chairman of the China Council for the Promotion of International Trade, the chairman of the All-China Federation of Commerce and Industry, and the director of the economics bureau of the State Council's Taiwan Office. At a press conference in Beijing on March 11, 1997, Tang Shubei said that the PRC departments concerned were formulating detailed rules and regulations for enforcing the "Law on Protecting Taiwan Investment."[27]

ROC leaders were ambivalent toward the strengthening of economic ties with mainland China. On the one hand, they recognized the desirability of creating interest groups on the mainland that would oppose the PRC threat to use force against Taiwan as being contrary to their interests. ROC officials knew that they could not prevent Taiwan entrepreneurs from investing in the mainland through overseas subsidiaries if they were determined to do so. Yet the Taiwan authorities feared that the island's economy would become too dependent on the mainland, that Taiwan's own industries would be "hollowed out," and that Taiwan businesspeople with investments on the mainland would be vulnerable to PRC political pressure.

As early as 1993 the ROC launched a "southward policy," encouraging Taiwan's entrepreneurs to invest in Southeast Asia rather than mainland China. Lee's "vacation trip" to the Philippines, Indonesia, and Thailand in 1994 had important economic as well as political purposes, as Lee stressed in his press conference on his return.[28] Shortly after Lee's trip to the Philippines, Economics Minister Chiang Pin-kung led a delegation of 140 businesspeople on a fact-finding visit to the former U.S. naval base at Subic Bay. The ROC had lent the Philippines $60 million to develop Subic Bay into an industrial zone, and Taiwan companies have become the leading investors there.[29]

ROC government and KMT enterprises have invested sizeable amounts in Southeast Asia, and the economic integration of Taiwan with Southeast Asia has been stimulated by reciprocal visits of economic officials, including cabinet ministers, and delegations of businesspeople. The "southward policy" has served the double purpose of strengthening Taiwan's economy and enhancing its international image. By the end of 1994 Taiwan had become the second largest investor in Southeast Asia, next to Japan, with cumulative investments of $21.6 billion, roughly equivalent to Taiwan's investments in mainland China.[30]

Despite official encouragement of investment in Southeast Asia, the region could not replace mainland China as a target for Taiwan investments. Proximity and the investors' familiarity with China's language and customs continued to exert a strong pull. ROC officials sought to slow the flow of investment by "jawboning" and by refusing to approve certain large-scale investment proposals. For example, in August 1996 Lee Teng-hui, in a speech to the National Assembly, said that the ROC should review the idea of using mainland China as a main market in the APROC project. Subsequent statements by Lee and senior economic officials indicated that Lee had not intended to withdraw the assertion in his six-point statement of April 1995 that Taiwan should make the mainland its economic hinterland. Nevertheless, it was clear that anxiety existed among ROC officials at the pace of Taiwan's investment on the mainland at a time when domestic investments had declined and the PRC refused to resume the Koo-Wang talks.[31] The Formosa Plastics Group promptly withdrew its application for approval of a $3 billion power plant project in Zhangzhou, Fujian. Subsequently, however, Y. C. Wang, chairman of the conglomerate, told the press that the project was going forward as a joint venture with a foreign company. He said that he could no longer afford to ignore the mainland's huge market and cheap labor.[32] In October 1997 PRC officials confirmed that the plant was being built.[33]

Official actions by the ROC during 1995–1996 demonstrated that despite misgivings regarding the growth of cross-strait trade and investment at a time of political tension with the PRC, the government itself was willing to take steps to further their expansion. For example, throughout this period the Ministry of Economic Affairs continued to approve individual mainland investment projects in amounts ranging from a few hundred thousand dollars to $26 million. In April 1996 the ministry issued regulations allowing businesspeople on the mainland to visit Taiwan for up to three months for training courses. In May 1996 the Mainland Affairs Council expanded the categories of professionals allowed to visit Taiwan to include legal, property, construction and media experts.[34] In June 1996 the MAC authorized Taiwan security brokerage houses, department stores, supermarkets, and freight handling services to invest in the PRC.[35] On July 1, 1996, the economics ministry eased restrictions on imports from the mainland, excluding only those on a "negative list" of 3,500 items, thus allowing the number of items permitted entry to increase from 2,917 to 3,900.[36] By November 1997 the number of approved import categories had increased to 5,365.[37]

Even government corporations engaged in trade or joint ventures with mainland entities during this period. The most striking such action was an agreement on July 11, 1996, by the China Petroleum Corporation (CPC) with the PRC's China National Offshore Oil Company

(CNOOC) to conduct joint exploration for oil in the South China Sea between Taiwan and Guangdong province.[38] The plan was put on hold, however, in October 1996 when the CPC abruptly canceled a meeting with the CNOOC in Beijing. The economics ministry had instructed the CPC and other government corporations to refrain from new overseas investments in order to channel funds into domestic investment. The CPC maintained a dialogue with its mainland partner, however, by sponsoring a conference in Kaohsiung on environmental protection in the petrochemical industry, attended by representatives of all three of the mainland's oil corporations. Earlier, the state-owned China Ship-building Corporation established an economic link with the mainland by ordering 3,000 tons of steel plates from the Chongqing Steel Co.[39]

In May 1998 the two governments revived the joint oil exploration project. *Xinhua* announced that the contract went into effect formally on May 1 and that the first phase would consist of a seismic survey at a cost of $1 million, to be shared equally by the two sides. The PRC spokesman called the project a major breakthrough in economic coop-eration between the two sides of the strait.[40]

Although the foregoing actions demonstrated that the ROC was pre-pared to allow a gradual increase in the economic integration of Tai-wan with mainland China, government officials continued to express concern lest the increase become too rapid or develop in ways that damaged Taiwan's economy. Lee's August 1, 1996, warning to private business was compressed into a frequently repeated policy slogan: "Avoid haste, be patient" (*jie ji yong ren*). Investors who had not regis-tered their investments with the government were granted a period of three months in which to register without penalty. By the end of the amnesty period, September 30, 1997, firms registered 7,739 investments totalling $2.91 billion. Those failing to register could be assessed fines ranging from $35,000 to $175,000.

Beginning July 1, 1997, the government banned mainland invest-ments in infrastructure, such as railways, highways, airports, power plants, and port facilities. Limits were placed on investments by large firms and single projects could not exceed $50 million. Small and me-dium firms, however, could invest without restraint.

Noneconomic Interchange

Although the trend toward economic integration was the strongest and most visible force drawing the two sides of the Taiwan Strait closer, many other forms of people-to-people exchanges were occurring. Many of these exchanges are listed and some are described in detail in the Straits Exchange Foundation's monthly publication *Chiao Liu* (*Exchanges*).

Certain exchanges served to underline the common cultural background of the people on the two sides of the strait. Museums mounted exhibits of traditional Chinese art. The famous porcelain center, Jingdezhen in Jiangxi province, sent an exhibit of its products to Taiwan. Performing artists presented Beijing opera and other forms of Chinese opera, as well as traditional folk songs and dances of the Han and minority peoples. Young experts in Chinese chess (*wei qi*) displayed their skills in Taiwan.

Exchanges were not limited to traditional arts. Dramatic troupes from each side presented modern plays. An exhibit of photographs of life in Taiwan toured the mainland. Cooks from Xian and Fuzhou demonstrated their specialties (including 108 ways of making steamed dumplings).

For the average person on Taiwan, a stronger bond to the mainland than traditional or modern arts is the folk religion practiced by large numbers of people in Taiwan and nearby Fujian province. In recent years, with Taiwan's growing prosperity, residents spent increasing amounts on building and refurbishing local temples and conducting religious festivals. In Fujian, also, the easing of communist controls has led to a revival of folk religion. The most popular deity in Taiwan is Mazu, the goddess of seafarers, whose place of origin, more than one thousand years ago, was the island of Meizhou in Fujian. Since 1987, when travel from Taiwan was legalized, thousands of believers have visited the Mazu temple in Meizhou and donated funds for its restoration. In May 1989, in defiance of the ban on direct travel to the mainland, three hundred fishermen sailed directly from Taiwan to Meizhou to celebrate Mazu's birthday. In January 1997 the ancient statue of Mazu from the Meizhou temple arrived in Taiwan aboard a chartered Eva Airways plane for a one-hundred-day tour of more than thirty Mazu temples throughout Taiwan, where it was worshiped by thousands of believers.

Buddhism has provided another link across the strait. In 1989 a prominent Buddhist leader, Master Xing Yun, founder of temples in Taiwan and the United States, led a three-hundred-member Buddhist delegation to the PRC where he met with Buddhist leaders and was received by Li Xiannian, chairman of the Chinese People's Political Consultative Conference, and by Zhu Rongji, mayor of Shanghai. The Tzu Chi Foundation, a Buddhist charitable organization of some two million members, that was established by a nun, Master Cheng Yen, (known as Taiwan's Mother Teresa), has engaged in disaster relief activities on the mainland. In 1991, for example, after a disastrous flood in Jiangsu, Anhui, and Henan, it donated $16 million for food, blankets, medicine, and housing construction for flood victims.[41]

Educational exchanges gathered momentum in 1996, despite the 1995–1996 military exercises. Wu Jin, the president of Cheng Kung University in Tainan, who later became minister of education, organized a meeting in January 1996 of the presidents of forty-three universities in Taiwan and mainland China to discuss higher education on the two sides of the strait and arrange faculty and student exchanges. In April of the same year fourteen high school principals from Beijing met with their counterparts in Taipei to compare notes on secondary education. Representatives of Hsinchu's Chiaotung University went to Shanghai to help celebrate the one-hundredth anniversary of the mother institution there. A delegation from Beijing's Qinghua University visited Tsinghua University in Hsinchu to strengthen bonds between these sister institutions. A delegation from PRC journalism schools went to Taiwan to exchange views with educators and practitioners in the field of journalism.

Since 1990 students from Taiwan have been admitted to universities on the mainland.[42] In 1997 some three to four thousand Taiwan students were studying there (including the son of the DPP chairman, Hsu Hsin-liang). For the tens of thousands who failed each year to pass the highly competitive entrance examinations for universities in Taiwan, study at a mainland university offered an inexpensive alternative, even though the government in Taipei refused to recognize mainland diplomas. Finally, in October 1997, the Ministry of Education in Taipei announced that it would recognize the degrees granted by seventy-three, or about 7 percent, of the mainland institutions of higher learning. The announcement provoked a storm of controversy. Senior KMT and DPP officials and legislators attacked the policy as exposing Taiwan students to PRC brainwashing. Education Minister Wu Jin stood by the decision, which had been studied for five years and approved by the MAC and the Executive Yuan. Premier Vincent Siew, however, reacting to the criticism, instructed the minister to work out the guidelines for implementing the decision with the MAC and to submit them to the Executive Yuan for approval.[43] As of mid-1998, the guidelines had not been approved.

The authorities on both sides of the strait have restricted the presence of media representatives from the other side. Both feared that correspondents might be used by the other side for political purposes.[44] Gradually, however, they both liberalized restrictions. By 1996 the PRC allowed Taiwan reporters to stay a maximum of one month. The *China Times* and the *Lien Ho Pao* always had a correspondent in Beijing, rotating them monthly; other Taiwan newspapers sent representatives frequently but did not maintain permanent representation. On the Taiwan side, PRC correspondents could stay for six months, but few stayed longer than two weeks. From 1989 to 1995 of the 103 PRC reporters who were given permission to enter Taiwan, 86 came.[45] In December 1996 the Executive Yuan was expected to approve a recommendation by the Mainland Affairs Council that mainland reporters be allowed to stay in Taiwan for up to two years. In addition to reporters, meetings held by representatives from the two sides of the strait included publishers, news agency directors, and editors.

Athletes traveled back and forth. In July 1994 Wang Jun, vice president of the China Golf Association and son of the late vice president of the PRC, Wang Zhen, led a group of golfers to discuss joint development of golf courses in mainland China.[46] Less than a month after the military exercises of March 1996, a women's volleyball team sponsored by the People's Liberation Army, arrived in Taiwan to compete against local teams. In October 1996 a dozen golfers from the mainland came to Taiwan to take part in matches. In March 1997 Wu Shaozu, minister of the Physical Culture and Sports Commission and president of the PRC's Olympic Committee, led a twenty-four-member delegation to Taiwan, including several medal-winners at the Atlanta Olympics. Wu, the most senior PRC official to visit Taiwan up to that time, met with Education Minister Wu Jin and stressed the importance of athletic exchanges.

Legal Immigration of Relatives

As indicated at the beginning of this chapter, the largest number of visitors from the mainland to Taiwan—more than forty thousand in 1996—were those who came to visit relatives. Taiwan residents born in mainland China could request approval for mainland parents, spouses, and children to visit them in Taiwan. Initially, permission was granted only to see sick relatives, but in 1995 the government lifted that limitation. In addition, it authorized qualified mainlanders to visit twice a year for a total stay of up to six months in a year.[47]

Travel to the mainland by tens of thousands of Taiwan businesspeople, some for lengthy stays, soon began to create new family connections between the two sides of the strait. Many Taiwan businesspeople satisfied their desire for female companionship by patronizing prostitutes or acquiring mistresses. One large shoe manufacturer sought to reduce the risk of undesirable liaisons by housing its 350 Taiwan managers in dormitories, sending their paychecks back home, and giving them home leave in Taiwan every two months.[48] Lengthy residence on the mainland, however, often resulted in Taiwan businessmen marrying mainland women; naturally, they wanted to be able to bring their wives into Taiwan. The ROC government, fearing a rash of "marriages of convenience" for the purpose of gaining residence in Taiwan, strictly limited the number of mainlanders granted permanent entry to join their spouses. Applicants had to have been married for at least two years or had to have a child. At first, the limit was 240 per year, but it was gradually increased until in May 1996 it was set at 1080 per year. Pressure for a further increase in the quota was strong, because 16,398 spouses were on the waiting list by late 1997.[49]

Fisheries Cooperation

For many years the owners of Taiwan fishingboats had coped with a shortage of fishermen in Taiwan by illegally hiring fishermen from the mainland.[50] Finally, in July 1995, the Council of Agriculture in Taiwan announced that boat owners could legally hire mainland fishermen for coastal fishing, as long as the vessels did not come within Taiwan's twelve-mile territorial sea limit. At that time an estimated 8,000 to 10,000 mainland fishermen were illegally employed on Taiwan vessels.[51] A PRC source stated that from October 1988 to the end of 1994, 88,692 mainland fishermen had been employed on Taiwan fishing vessels.[52]

Another example of increased Taiwan-mainland fisheries interaction was a two-day seminar in Taipei in May 1996, attended by a twenty-nine-member delegation from the mainland to exchange views on cross-strait fisheries cooperation.[53]

Illegal Activities

Some of the people-to-people relations that developed across the strait were less constructive than those discussed in previous passages. These were illegal activities, such as illegal immigration, smuggling, counterfeiting, extortion, and hijacking of aircraft. Yet, paradoxically, they forced the two governments to find ways of cooperating.[54]

In 1990 the Red Cross Societies of the two sides reached an agreement in Chinmen (Quemoy) to repatriate people who sneaked into Taiwan illegally and persons wanted for crimes on either side. By the end of 1997 35,262 illegal immigrants had been apprehended and 34,638 repatriated.[55] As of January 1998, some 400 were being held in Taiwan's detention centers, a low figure compared to previous years.[56]

Authorities on both sides were becoming increasingly concerned with the rise in crime and growing collaboration between criminal gangs in Taiwan and those on the China mainland. Some progress was made in arresting and deporting those accused of crimes. During the six years after the Chinmen Agreement, the PRC deported thirty-four criminal suspects to Taiwan and Taiwan deported seven to the mainland. ROC officials, however, criticized the PRC for not being active enough in tracking down and arresting suspects. In November 1996 the ROC's Justice Minister, Liao Cheng-ho, who was pressing a campaign to round up gang leaders in Taiwan, appealed to the PRC authorities for help in locating and arresting over one hundred wanted criminals thought to have fled to the mainland. The ROC, which had been unwilling to permit direct contact between police officials on the two sides of the strait, now saw many advantages in cross-strait official visits and communication.[57] By late 1997 further progress had been made. A SEF spokesman reported that of the 198 criminals or suspects whose arrest had been requested through ARATS, 46 had been repatriated by the end of September 1997. He added, "There are many ongoing cooperation projects in criminal investigation between the two sides."[58]

In April 1997, after a lengthy hiatus, the PRC Red Cross officials turned over to the ROC Red Cross three criminal suspects from Taiwan who had fled to the mainland and received seven illegal immigrants arrested by the police in Chinmen. Later in the same month, Lee Ching-ping, the deputy secretary-general of SEF, made a five-day visit to Beijing, where he met with ARATS vice chairman Tang Shubei and discussed with Justice Ministry officials methods of improving cooperation in fighting crime and in repatriating fugitives from justice.[59]

On March 10, 1997, a hijacker forced a plane on a Taiwan domestic flight to fly to Xiamen, where he was arrested by the local authorities, who promptly refueled the plane and allowed it to go on to Taipei with its crew and passengers. The PRC at first refused Taipei's request to send the hijacker to Taiwan for trial on the grounds that the Taiwan authorities had refused to send back to the mainland sixteen hijackers previously jailed in Taiwan. Eventually, however, the PRC returned the hijacker to Taiwan, where he was given a life sentence, and the ROC sent to the mainland two of the sixteen hijackers, who had completed their jail sentence in Taiwan.

The need for the two sides to work together to suppress crime is becoming increasingly obvious but has been obstructed by the suspension of talks through the Koo-Wang channel, where a consensus had been reached in May 1995 on the treatment of hijackers, among other topics, but no agreement had been signed. The signing of agreements on handling crime is difficult because it raises questions related to the

conflicting views on the extent of Taiwan's jurisdiction and the author-
ity of its courts—issues that ultimately bring up the issue of sovereignty.

Integrative and Divisive Forces

The outstanding characteristics of the regional environment in which
Taiwan seeks to survive and prosper are rapid economic growth and
increasing interdependence. Mainland China has become a central factor in this economic transformation. In 1996 it attracted some $42 bil-
lion, more than one-third of all worldwide investment in manufacturing plants in developing countries.[60] Because Taiwan's prosperity
depends on foreign trade and international competitiveness, it cannot
avoid being drawn more deeply into mainland China's orbit. In their
drive to expand their market share in the global economy, Taiwan's
large transnational conglomerates, as well as many small and medium-
sized firms that are dependent on foreign trade, must enter into fierce
competition with their rivals for a share of the China market and the
use of China as a base for exports.

The integrative power of cross-strait trade and investment depends
on China's continued economic growth and the ability of Taiwan's entrepreneurs to take advantage of opportunities there. Not every investor has been successful. Some have lost money and, in a few extreme
cases, have been robbed or kidnapped. Yet the attraction remains
strong, as evidenced by the determination of leading Taiwan corporations to expand their activities on the mainland. During 1997 the flow
of trade and investment appeared to be recovering from the slowdown
caused by the military confrontation of 1995–1996.

Not only do Taiwan firms benefit from their access to the China
mainland but so do their joint venture partners and local and provincial officials, particularly those in areas where Taiwan investment is
most heavily concentrated, such as Fujian, Guangdong, Shanghai, and
Jiangsu. Officials in those cities and provinces presumably use their influence on the central government to adopt policies congenial to this
economic activity and to avoid actions that would adversely affect it.
But it is unclear how much influence these local officials may have in
Beijing on such issues. Business leaders in Taiwan do have considerable influence on the ROC's cross-strait economic policy, but even their
influence is limited, as is demonstrated by the variety of restrictions
applied to cross-strait interaction, particularly the government's weak-
ening but still evident determination to require that cross-strait travel
and investment be indirect.

Cross-strait economic relations clearly benefit a large number of individuals on both sides of the strait and influence governments toward cooperation rather than conflict. Both governments rely heavily on economic development to strengthen their positions in the international arena. The cross-strait relationship contributes significantly to economic development, although it is much more important to Taiwan's small economy than to the mainland's large one. A paradox for the PRC is that the economic relationship, which it does much to encourage, has the effect of strengthening Taiwan's position in the global economy, which the ROC then uses to enhance its international political stature. Thus, both governments see risks as well as gains in the economic relationship, but driven as it is primarily by the profit motives of individuals and corporations, as long as healthy growth prevails in the economies concerned, this will continue to be the strongest bond between the two sides of the strait and the tendency will be for it to become still stronger.

The impact of noneconomic forms of cross-strait interaction is more difficult to judge than mutually beneficial economic activities. For example, do visits to the mainland by tourists incline them more toward cooperation with the PRC or toward an increased appreciation of Taiwan's separateness? On the one hand, they are reminded of the linguistic, cultural, and historical affinities between Taiwan and mainland China. On the other hand, they are exposed directly to the mainland's much lower living standard. Poorer relations often pressure their Taiwanese relatives for handouts. Instead of drawing the two peoples closer together, contacts may result in cultivating a sense of superiority among Taiwanese visitors and envy on the part of the mainlanders.

Exchanges between professionals with interests in common are probably more effective than tourism in fostering a spirit of cooperation and lasting personal and institutional relationships. There are many areas in which cooperation confers benefits on individuals and institutions on both sides. Those who benefit from this form of cooperation are mostly the educated elite, some of whom have contacts with policymakers, whom they seek to influence toward cross-strait cooperation rather than confrontation.

It seems evident that the positive aspects of cross-strait, people-to-people relationships far outweigh the negative ones. This positive interaction served to temper the downward spiral in political relations that followed Lee Teng-hui's Cornell visit but could not prevent it. The crux of the political difference between Beijing and Taipei, as discussed in Chapter 3, is the former's insistence that Taiwan is part of the PRC and the latter's insistence that it is not. The principal means by which the Taipei authorities demonstrate that Taiwan is not a part of the PRC is through cultivating its independent relationships with foreign countries, some of them formal diplomatic relations, but most of them unofficial or quasi-official. Lee Teng-hui has sought to expand Taiwan's "international living space" by his pragmatic diplomacy, which consists of strengthening Taiwan's substantive relations with other countries and, wherever possible, moving them closer to an official level. It is this "creeping officiality" that has so disturbed the PRC and has convinced PRC leaders that Lee secretly backs Taiwan independence, despite his public commitment to the eventual unification of Taiwan with mainland China. Lee's pragmatic diplomacy is, in part, a response to pressure on him by the DPP, which openly opposes unification and favors Taiwan independence. The next chapter discusses pragmatic diplomacy, how it relates to democratic politics in Taiwan, and how it contributes to political strain between the PRC and Taiwan.

Notes

1. Mainland Affairs Council, Taipei, *Beyond the Historical Gap: Retrospect and Prospect of Ten Years' Cross-Strait Exchanges* (1997), p. 369.

2. These are contracted amounts, as reported by Beijing. Remitted amounts may be only half these figures: $10 billion–$15 billion. *Far Eastern Economic Review* (October 10, 1996): 50–52).

3. Mainland Affairs Council, Taipei, *MAC News Briefing*, no. 0046, (October 27, 1997): 1.

4. Survey of 1384 local firms conducted by *United Daily News* and *Economic Daily News*, reported in *China Post*, (October 4, 1995).

5. *China Post* (May 17, 1995).

6. *China Post* (August 11, 1995).

7. *China Post* (February 10, 1996).

8. Chu Yun-han, "Cross-Strait Dilemma," *Free China Review*, vol. 47, no. 6 (June 1997): 45.

9. *People's Daily, Overseas Edition* (August 30, 1996).

10. *Free China Journal* (September 20, 1996).

11. *China Post* (December 23, 1996).

12. *China Post* (January 30, 1997).

13. *Far Eastern Economic Review* (February 15, 1996): 45.

14. *Free China Journal* (October 9, 1997).

15. *Free China Journal* (June 5, 1998).

16. *China Post* (March 20, 1997).

17. *China Post* (May 15, 1995; November 13, 1996).

18. *China Post* (July 19; September 11, 1996); *New York Times* (March 4, 1997).

19. *Free China Journal* (March 28, 1997).

20. *China Post* (April 27, 1996); *New York Times* (March 4, 1997).

21. According to the Institute of Information Industry, Taipei, *Free China Journal* (December 5, 1997).

22. *Free China Journal* (January 23, 1998).

23. *FBIS* (February 5, 1996): 70.

24. *China Post* (March 3, 1997).

25. Wang Hui, deputy director of the Taiwan–Hong Kong–Macau Department of the Ministry of Foreign Trade and Economic Cooperation, cited in Taipei's *Hsin Hsin Wen* (January 5, 1997): 84.

26. Council on Economic Planning and Development, cited in *China Post* (March 3, 1997).

27. *Wen Wei Po* (March 12, 1997).

28. *Chung Yang Jih Pao*, February 18, 1994 (in *FBIS* [Feb. 24, 1994]: 58–63).

29. *Free China Journal* (February 25, 1994); *Far Eastern Economic Review* (July 15, 1993): 13.

30. Lee Teng-hui's state of the union address, July 27, 1995 (in *FBIS* [August 2, 1995]: 74).

31. *China Post* (August 16, 17, 1996).

32. *China Post* (March 31, 1997).

33. *China Post* (October 24, 1997).

34. *China Post* (April 17; May 28, 1996).

35. *China Post* (June 19, 1996).

36. *Free China Journal* (April 19, 1996).

37. Taiwan: Central News Agency (November 11, 1997 via World News Connection [*FBIS*]).

38. *Free China Journal* (July 19, 1996); Lou Tzu-chiang, "Liang An Shi You Gong Ye Kai Chuang He Zuo Xin Qi Ji" ("Petroleum Industries of the Two Sides of the Strait Create a New Opportunity for Cooperation"), *Chiao Liu*, 29, (September 1996): 35–38.

39. *Central News Agency*, August 2, 1995 (in *FBIS* [August 2, 1995]: 80).

40. *China Post* (June 1, 1998).

41. Government Information Office, Taipei, *The Republic of China Yearbook, 1993*, p. 509.

42. Clough, *Reaching*, pp. 89–90.

43. Mainland Affairs Council, Taipei, *MAC News Briefing* no. 0049 (November 17, 1997): 1; *Free China Journal* (November 28, 1997).

44. Clough, *Reaching*, pp. 80–89.

45. *Free China Journal* (May 5, 1995).

46. *China Post* (July 21, 1994). In 1997 Wang Jun gained notoriety in the United States for having attended a coffee get-together in the White House hosted by President Clinton. Wang was president of the PRC's leading investment conglomerate, the China International Trust and Investment Corporation (CITIC), as well as a military-owned arms trading company under investigation for illegal smuggling of assault rifles into the United States. *Washington Post* (March 16, 1997).

47. *China Post* (March 15, 1995).

48. The firm was Yue Yuen Industrial Holdings, a Taiwan-owned firm regis-

tered in Hong Kong that had 54,000 employees in Guangdong making sports shoes for Nike, Reebok, and Adidas. *Far Eastern Economic Review* (August 1, 1996): 50–51.

49. *China Post* (March 15, April 16, May 31, 1996; November 6, 1997).

50. Clough, *Reaching,* pp. 74–76.

51. *China Post* (July 31, 1995).

52. *Fujian Ribao,* August 31, 1995 (in *FBIS* [September 25, 1995]: 70).

53. *Central News Agency,* Taiwan, May 31, 1996 (in *FBIS* [May 31, 1996]: 82).

54. Clough, *Reaching,* Chap. 4, pp. 63–76.

55. Mac, *Beyond the Historical Gap,* p. 367.

56. *China Post* (January 24, 1998).

57. *China Post* (November 16, 1996); Chang Chung-yung, professor at the Central Police Academy in Taiwan, "Zheng Shi Liang An Gong Tong Da Ji Fan Zui Di Wen T'i." ("Focus on the Issue of a Joint Attack on Crime by the Two Sides of the Strait"), *Chiao Liu,* 31, (January 1997): 25–27.

58. Mainland Affairs Council, Taipei, *MAC News Briefing* No. 0048 (November 10, 1997): 1.

59. *China Post* (April 17, 30, 1997).

60. *New York Times* (March 24, 1997).

Chapter 5

Pragmatic Diplomacy and Democratic Politics

For both governments the advantages of people-to-people relations across the Taiwan Strait outweigh the disadvantages. The prospects for Taiwan and mainland China to live peaceably, side by side—whatever their ultimate political relationship may be—will clearly be improved by a growing network of personal and institutional connections. The motives of the two governments in permitting or encouraging people-to-people relations differ, and they disagree concerning the pace and manner in which they should develop, but both approve substantial growth in such relations.

The crux of their differences lies not in cross-strait relations but in Taiwan's relations with the outside world. The PRC wants the world to accept its view that relations between mainland China and Taiwan are a domestic matter and that only the central government has the right to determine what the nature of Taiwan's relations with the outside world should be. PRC leaders say that they have no objection to Taiwan's economic and cultural relations with other countries, but they object adamantly to diplomatic and official relations and to the use of the term "Republic of China."

Taiwan authorities reject any limitation on the freedom of the "Republic of China" to establish diplomatic or official relationships with other countries. They deny that the PRC has any right to prescribe the nature of Taiwan's foreign relations. Taiwan functions in the world as a de facto sovereign state, relying on its growing economic power to demonstrate to the world that it deserves to be treated like any other independent country.

The only impediment to Taiwan's being treated like other independent countries is the PRC's opposition. PRC leaders are determined to prevent Taiwan from gaining de jure recognition as an independent state. The PRC is so large and powerful and the lure of its market so compelling that few countries have been willing to challenge it by establishing official relations with Taiwan at the cost of losing diplomatic relations with Beijing and access to the China market.

Bilateral Diplomatic Relations

The PRC has effectively isolated the ROC in terms of bilateral diplomatic relations. In mid-1998, of the 185 UN members, the ROC had diplomatic relations with only 27. All of them were small states, mostly in Africa, the Caribbean, Latin America, and the South Pacific.[1]

Despite the odds against it, the ROC did not abandon the struggle to increase the number of its diplomatic partners. Between 1989 and 1992 it established diplomatic relations with eight countries in Africa and the Caribbean region with which the PRC already had diplomatic relations, causing Beijing to break relations with those countries.[2] The PRC struck back by restoring its suspended relations with Indonesia, establishing relations with Singapore, and winning over Saudi Arabia and South Korea, two of the three remaining sizeable countries with which the ROC still had diplomatic relations.

In 1988 and 1989 the ROC established an International Cooperation and Development Fund and an International Humanitarian and Relief Fund as instruments for expanding its role and enhancing its image in the world. By March 1996 the two funds had disbursed a total of $613 million, $125 million of this in the form of disaster relief. The ROC has sent forty-seven technical cooperation teams to thirty-three countries to provide agricultural, technical, and medical assistance.[3] In providing economic aid, the ROC has given priority to solidifying existing relationships with diplomatic partners, but aid offers have at times been useful in luring small countries away from the PRC's fold. The ROC's aid program is not large, however, less than 0.1 percent of the GNP, which is far below the 0.7 percent set as a target for industrial states by the United Nations.[4]

In some places the PRC probably outbid the ROC in offers of economic aid, but for the most part it could rely on its more imposing image as the most populous state in the world, a nuclear power, and one of the five permanent members of the UN Security Council. It was also an active member of the world's most important intergovernmental organizations, from which the ROC was excluded. A small state must have very special reasons to choose Taipei over Beijing when the United States, Japan, the countries of western Europe, and all of the other principal industrialized countries have chosen to have diplomatic relations with the big China rather than the small China.

A retired ROC diplomat, Bernard Joei, turned the spotlight on the diplomatic rivalry in Africa between Taipei and Beijing during 1996 and early 1997. During 1996, Joei says, nineteen PRC officials of vice-minister rank or higher visited twenty-seven of the fifty-three African states and the PRC received ten African leaders on state visits. In January 1997 the ROC foreign minister, John Chang, seeking to counteract these PRC activities and the impending loss of diplomatic relations with South Africa, visited seven of the nine African states (including South Africa), with which the ROC had diplomatic relations. The PRC countered by sending its foreign minister, Qian Qichen, to visit five of its diplomatic partners in Africa.[5]

In May 1997 the ROC announced the establishment of diplomatic relations with a West African island state, the Democratic Republic of Sao Tome and Principe, with a population variously reported as 127,000 or 140,000. Since 1975 this small country had depended heavily on economic aid from the PRC, accumulating a debt of some $28 million. The ROC, in establishing diplomatic relations, promised aid of $30 million over a ten-year period and paid $4.3 million as a first installment. The PRC was taken by surprise, because Foreign Minister Qian Qichen had visited Sao Tome and Principe in January 1997 and had signed another aid agreement. Beijing warned that the link with Taiwan endangered ties with Beijing but did not immediately sever relations, since the parliament of the island country voted against the president's decision to establish relations with the ROC.[6] As of mid-1998, the domestic struggle over the establishment of relations with the ROC was still going on and diplomats from both Beijing and Taipei were in Sao Tome pressing their cause.

The battle in Africa was particularly tense in 1997 because the PRC, after losing Gambia and Senegal to the ROC in 1995 and 1996, won back Niger in August 1996 and took the big prize, South Africa, in December.[7] ROC authorities feared that the PRC would redouble its efforts in Africa in the hope that the victory in South Africa would cause the remainder of the ROC's diplomatic partners to move into the PRC's camp. Clearly, the PRC was working hard to bring about the total exclusion of the ROC's diplomatic presence from the African continent, but success was not a foregone conclusion, for in August and September 1997 Taipei announced the reestablishment of relations with Chad and Liberia, causing the PRC to break its ties with both countries.

The diplomatic struggle between Taipei and Beijing also heated up during 1997 in Central America and the Caribbean. Fourteen of the ROC's diplomatic partners were in this region, including those that annually sponsored the proposal to include the Taiwan issue in the agenda of the UN General Assembly. In his first trip abroad since his Cornell visit, Lee challenged the PRC by attending an international conference on the Panama Canal in Panama City September 7–10, 1997, took part in a summit meeting of the heads of state of all six Central American countries, and made state visits to Honduras and Paraguay.

The PRC could not dissuade Panama from inviting Lee, but its outspoken opposition to Lee's presence at the conference affected the level of representation. Aside from Lee and President Perez Balladares of Panama, the only heads of state from the forty-one countries participating came from Honduras and Nicaragua. The United States sent Transportation Secretary Rodney Slater and President Clinton's special envoy for Latin American and Caribbean Affairs, Thomas F. McLarty. The PRC, one of the leading users of the canal, boycotted the conference, as did the United Nations.[8]

Whatever luster Lee's trip may have produced for pragmatic diplomacy was dimmed by diplomatic gains by the PRC in Central America and the Caribbean. In May 1997 the PRC won diplomatic recognition from the Bahamas, after a Hong Kong conglomerate, Hutchison Whampoa, agreed to invest $175 million in refurbishing hotels and constructing a container port there. Unable to persuade the Bahamas to reverse its decision and worried about a possible domino effect on nearby countries, the ROC severed diplomatic relations.[9]

In August 1997, after the government of St. Lucia, an island state of 145,000 people, announced its intention to establish relations with Beijing, the ROC broke off diplomatic relations and ended its agricultural and other cooperation programs. The opening of PRC trade offices in Panama and Haiti, despite ROC protests, aroused fears that these moves were precursors to a switch of diplomatic relations to Beijing, as had happened in South Africa, after the PRC was permitted to open a representative office there in 1992.

The PRC ambassador to the United Nations, Qin Huasun, vigorously cultivated governments in Central America and the Caribbean that had diplomatic relations with the ROC. In April 1997 he visited St. Kitts and Nevis and Costa Rica, at the invitation of those governments. In Costa Rica the PRC was reported to have agreed to purchase annually significant quantities of sugar and coffee, in an attempt to overcome the advantage gained by the ROC's $50 million loan to that country in 1996.[10] Qin's July 1997 visit to St. Lucia, at which he reportedly offered to contribute $1 million to an education fund and promised investments in public works, preceded that government's decision to switch diplomatic relations to Beijing.[11]

The PRC used sticks as well as carrots in its campaign to cause small countries to break relations with the ROC. Its leaders gave notice that diplomatic partners of the ROC would no longer be permitted to have consulates in Hong Kong after July 1, 1997. Consequently, St. Kitts and Nevis, Senegal, Tonga, the Dominican Republic, Panama, Costa Rica, Paraguay, the Central African Republic, and Belize all closed their consulates in Hong Kong. Tonga, Belize, and the Dominican Republic replaced their consulates with unofficial trade offices and some of the other states may accept this reduced status.[12]

Beijing also used its position on the Security Council as a diplomatic weapon against the ROC. In January 1997 it vetoed a Security Council measure that would provide UN observers to monitor the cease-fire reached between the Guatemalan government and rebel forces, the first veto ever cast by the PRC. After tense negotiations, the PRC agreed to withdraw the veto, reportedly in exchange for Guatemala's promise not to support in 1997 the proposal for consideration by the UN General Assembly of UN participation by Taiwan.[13] Thus, the PRC is becoming more inventive in finding ways to pressure those few countries that continue to maintain diplomatic relations with the ROC.

Quasi-Official Relations

For a long time ROC leaders have recognized that they cannot compete with the PRC in the arena of diplomatic relations. Beijing holds the high cards. In order to carry on Taiwan's economic and cultural relations with other countries, they have been forced to improvise, employing a broad range of unconventional methods to substitute for their lack of diplomatic relations. On the whole, Taiwan's informal diplomacy has been quite successful in enabling the people of Taiwan to travel and trade throughout the world and to constantly expand the operations of Taiwan-owned airlines, shipping companies, fisheries, and transnational corporations.

Taiwan has exchanged ostensibly unofficial missions with all of its principal trading partners, which serve in most respects as surrogate embassies. Those in Taipei (forty-seven as of 1995) are often headed by retired ambassadors or other senior officials temporarily separated from their official positions. These missions have increased in number, size, and scope of functions as the importance of Taiwan's role in the world has increased. As of 1995 the ROC had set up official or quasi-official offices in sixty-five countries with which it lacked diplomatic relations. Fourteen of these countries allowed Taipei to use the name "Republic of China," despite Beijing's protests. Although relatively few countries have been willing to brave the PRC's wrath by allowing the ROC to name its offices abroad with its official title, most of them, including the United States and Japan, have agreed in recent years to replace a disguised appellation with a recognizable title, now most commonly "The Taipei Economic and Cultural Office."[14] In addition to the offices abroad maintained by the foreign ministry, the China External Trade Development Council (CETRA), jointly funded by the government and private business, has thirty-eight offices in twenty-eight countries.

The PRC's policy toward Taiwan contains a fundamental contradiction. PRC leaders profess to have no objection to Taiwan's economic and cultural relations with foreign countries, but they object vehemently to official relationships. Yet without such relationships, it would be impossible for any country to have extensive economic and cultural relations in the modern world. Governments must agree on the ground rules for trade, travel, shipping, air services, and a host of other things if the people and institutions of two countries are to freely interact with each other. The result has been Taiwan's resort to a multitude of devices to obscure official participation in concluding agreements, so as to make it easier for other governments to assure the PRC that relations with Taiwan are unofficial. To Beijing's dismay, this charade became increasingly common and transparent, but so many countries were involved that it was impossible for the PRC to prevent Taiwan's international relations from inching closer to a patently official level.[15]

The ROC has cemented its bilateral relations through the exchange of visits by high-level officials. Where visits by presidents, premiers, or foreign ministers were considered likely to provoke a strong PRC reaction, the ROC has exchanged officials of cabinet rank, usually in the economic field. For example, an early breakthrough was the visit to Taiwan in January 1991 of the French Minister of Trade and Territorial Development, Roger Fauroux, heading a delegation of twenty-eight government officials and business leaders.[16] French firms were attracted by the ROC's 1991–1996 development plan, originally projecting the expenditure of $300 billion. The French hoped to land large contracts to build a nuclear power plant, subways, and a high-speed railway. Fauroux's visit was followed by trade ministers from other European countries. Ministerial visits by the ROC to its European and other trading partners became increasingly common. The governments involved brushed aside PRC protests by asserting that the exchanges were "unofficial." The more important Taiwan's economic relations with its partners became, the more willing they were to exchange high-level visits, despite the PRC's opposition.

More troubling to Beijing than Taipei's exchanges of visits by cabinet ministers with its trading partners was Lee Teng-hui's travel abroad. Chiang Ching-kuo never left Taiwan after he became president, but Lee had completed barely a year in office as Chiang's successor when he visited Singapore in March 1989, taking with him fourteen cabinet ministers and forty media representatives. At that time Singapore did not have diplomatic relations with either Taipei or Beijing. When Lee returned, he told the press that he was willing to visit other countries, even those that had diplomatic relations with the PRC.

In 1994 Lee inaugurated "vacation diplomacy," following up a visit by Premier Lien Chan to Malaysia and Singapore with visits to the Philippines, Indonesia, and Thailand. Lee took with him senior officials and leading businesspeople and met with President Ramos, President Suharto, and the King of Thailand. In 1995 he visited Jordan and the United Arab Emirates, shortly before his visit to Cornell. After his election in March 1996, Lee was preoccupied with constitutional reforms and domestic politics and did not travel abroad until his September 1997 trip to Panama. Beijing's military response to Lee's Cornell visit probably has caused countries to be more cautious in receiving his private visits.[17]

Taiwan's economic prowess has enabled the ROC to advance vigorously in consolidating its substantive bilateral relations. The flow of trade and capital and the travel back and forth by Taiwan officials and their counterparts, even at the cabinet level, cannot be seriously impeded by the PRC. These activities receive relatively low-level media attention. Visits by the premier or president are another matter. They are conducted primarily to heighten the image of the ROC as an international actor. Consequently, they attract considerable media attention and stimulate the PRC to take countermeasures.

It could be argued that the ROC can accomplish most of what it needs in relations with the rest of the world without visits at the highest levels, but Taiwan's democratic politics make it difficult for political leaders to refrain from such visits. Not only do they contribute to the leader's popularity, but they also help him to refute the view propounded by the DPP that only by declaring Taiwan an independent republic, separate from China, can it gain the respect and dignity it deserves in the world community. Lee and mainstream opinion in Taiwan also assert that the more extensive Taiwan's relationships with foreign countries, the stronger its negotiating position on political issues with the PRC.

International Governmental Organizations

Since the PRC acquired the China seat in the United Nations in 1971, compelling the ROC to withdraw, PRC leaders have opposed the

ROC's membership in intergovernmental organizations (IGOs). The PRC has forced the ROC out of all IGOs affiliated with the United Nations and nearly all others, on the ground that Taiwan is not a sovereign state. Exceptional circumstances and support by the United States and other major powers enabled Taiwan to retain its membership in the Asian Development Bank (ADB), under the name "Taipei, China" and to join the Asia-Pacific Cooperation group (APEC) under the name "Chinese-Taipei." In the latter, however, the ROC can be represented only by its economics minister, rather than the foreign minister, and Lee Teng-hui has been excluded from APEC heads of state meetings.

Taiwan has also applied to join the World Trade Organization as "the Separate Customs Territory of Taiwan, Penghu, Chinmen and Matsu." By the end of 1997, Taiwan appeared close to meeting the conditions for membership, but the PRC, which had applied earlier, still faced significant obstacles. Members of the organization seemed prepared to meet the PRC's demand that Taiwan not be admitted first.

The ROC's primary challenge to the PRC in the international arena has been its campaign for participation in the UN General Assembly. Lee Teng-hui at first opposed as impractical this idea put forward by the DPP and supported by a resolution passed by the Legislative Yuan in 1991, because the PRC, as a permanent member of the Security Council, had the power to veto new members. However, when the DPP made UN entry its main foreign policy issue and was gaining increasing public support, Lee decided to make it a long-range policy goal for the ROC. Since September 1993 a handful of the ROC's diplomatic partners in Central America have sponsored each year a resolution calling for including in the agenda of the UN General Assembly the issue of Taiwan's participation.[18]

The PRC, of course, firmly opposed any discussion in the UN of Taiwan's participation, and it has succeeded in keeping the item off the UN General Assembly's agenda. PRC officials regularly cite the ROC's UN campaign as further evidence that Lee Teng-hui is a secret supporter of an independent Taiwan. Taipei contends that the ROC's membership in the United Nations, following the precedents of the two Germanys and the two Koreas, would improve, not detract from, prospects for unification. It rejects the DPP's view that Taiwan should be admitted as a new state: "the Republic of Taiwan."

Although the ROC has little chance of gaining entry to the United Nations as long as the PRC is opposed, its lobbying of UN members and its extensive publicity have made Taiwan better known in the world community. The ROC can easily demonstrate that it has all the qualifications for UN membership and would have no difficulty winning acceptance if the PRC should withdraw its opposition. But the failure of the campaign to make any discernible progress toward getting the Taiwan issue on the UN agenda has caused some commentators in Taiwan to question its value. For example, a former KMT legislator, Wei Yung, argues that the drive for UN membership should be slackened. "Why should we do something that has little chance of success and also irritates mainland China so much? It seems we are losing both ways."[19]

The ROC foreign ministry, unable to make progress toward ROC participation in the UN General Assembly, turned its attention to certain UN-affiliated IGOs, whose regulations offered better prospects for Taiwan's participation and where the PRC had no veto power. In April 1997 the ROC requested observer status at the World Health Assembly, scheduled for May 5 in Geneva. The World Health Organization rejected the request on the grounds that observer status was reserved for certain noncontroversial nongovernmental organizations such as the International Committee of the Red Cross. The ROC foreign minister indicated that Taiwan would continue to seek observer status in other IGOs that were more technical than political.[20]

International Nongovernmental Organizations

Excluded from nearly all IGOs, Taiwan has vigorously sought participation in international nongovernmental organizations (INGOs), the members of which are not governments but individuals or private groups. Even in these organizations, however, people from Taiwan have had to contend with PRC efforts either to exclude them or to insist on the use of a name that implies a status subordinate to that of the mainland Chinese participants.

Soon after the PRC became a UN member, it secured passage of a resolution in the United Nations Educational, Scientific, and Cultural Organization (UNESCO), calling on all of the 319 INGOs then associated with UNESCO to sever their ties with "bodies or elements linked with Chiang Kai-shek." Most of the 38 INGOs that had representatives from Taiwan declined to expel them, on the grounds that they were nonpolitical organizations. The PRC continued to press, if not for the expulsion of representatives from Taiwan, at least to prevent them from using the name "Republic of China" or otherwise identifying Taiwan as a region distinct from China. Because most members of INGOs wanted participants from both the PRC and Taiwan, over a period of time they worked out formulas for names that both Beijing and Taipei could accept.[21]

One of the longest running battles between Beijing and Taipei concerning membership in an INGO was over the Olympic Games. This contest began in 1952 and was not finally resolved until 1984, when Taipei accepted the compromise proposed by the International Olympic Committee and took part alongside the PRC in the Los Angeles Olympic Games under the name "Chinese Taipei" and using newly devised substitutes for the ROC's national flag and anthem. Many individual sports federations adopted the "Olympic formula" so that by 1987 Beijing belonged to twenty-eight international sports federations and Taipei belonged to twenty-seven.

A similar compromise on nomenclature led to the membership of both Beijing and Taipei in the International Council of Scientific Unions (ICSU). In 1982 the ICSU General Assembly designated "China" as the sole member country but represented by two adhering organizations: the "China Association for Science and Technology, Beijing" and the "Academy of Science located in Taipei, China." The "ICSU formula" was subsequently adopted by specialized scientific unions. For example, in the International Union of Pharmacology the participants are designated: "Chinese Pharmacological Society (Beijing)" and "Chinese Pharmacological Society (Taipei)." In the International Astronomical Union they are designated: "Chinese Astronomical Society, Nanjing" and "Astronomy Union located at Taipei, China." As of 1987, both Beijing and Taipei were represented in sixteen of these scientific unions.[22]

Other INGOs have adopted the "Olympic formula" in order to permit both Beijing and Taipei to become members. For example, both are members of the Pacific Economic Cooperation Conference (PECC), with participants from government, business, and academia. The PRC national committee is called the "China National Committee for Pacific Economic Cooperation" and the ROC's national committee goes by the name of "Chinese-Taipei Pacific Economic Cooperation Committee."

The PRC has shown particular sensitivity in regard to INGOs that deal with security issues. For example, it tried to prevent a Rome-based organization, the International School on Disarmament and Research on Conflict (ISODARCO) from holding an international conference in Taipei in April 1995, threatening to ban future ISODARCO conferences from Beijing if the Taipei conference were held. ISODARCO nevertheless went ahead with the conference. European and American scholars took part, but Beijing refused to permit Chinese scholars to participate. Another INGO concerned with security issues is the Council on Security Cooperation in Asia and the Pacific (CSCAP). Composed of scholars from countries of the region and officials attending meetings as observers in their private capacity, its members wanted to admit scholars from the PRC and Taiwan. Lengthy discussions among those concerned finally reached a compromise. Think-tanks in the United States, Japan, China, South Korea, and the ASEAN countries organized CSCAP committees composed of individuals interested in security issues, who became members of CSCAP. Scholars in Taiwan were not allowed to become members but could attend working committee meetings as individuals.

The acceptance of compromises on nomenclature permitted both Beijing and Taipei to belong to a large number of INGOs. As of 1992, the PRC belonged to 865 and Taiwan to 695. Interestingly, Hong Kong belonged to 884 and, according to the Sino-British Joint Declaration of 1984, it may continue to participate in these international organizations as part of the PRC.[23]

Domestic Politics and Foreign Policy

Taiwan's future is being shaped by two complex, rapidly evolving trends: its changing relationship with mainland China and its changing relationship with the rest of the world. Both of these trends are increasingly affected by the workings of domestic politics in Taiwan.

The roots of the political opposition movement in Taiwan reach back to the oppressive climate of 1945–1947 that culminated in the brutal killing of opposition leaders after the riots of February 28, 1947. The KMT, initially welcomed as Chinese compatriots freeing the people of Taiwan from Japanese colonialism, came to be seen by most Taiwanese as a repressive outside force. Thus, the opposition, which coalesced into the Democratic Progressive Party in 1986, sought not only to replace the KMT as the ruling party but also to turn Taiwan into an independent state, governed by the people of Taiwan. As the opposition gained strength, however, the KMT itself was becoming increasingly Taiwanese. Even Chiang Kai-shek, whose goal in the 1950s was to prepare a mainlander-dominated KMT to recover the mainland, recognized that to rule over the antagonized Taiwanese people, who constituted 85 percent of the island's population, the KMT would have to bring many of them into the party. Over the next three decades, while Chiang Kai-shek and Chiang Ching-kuo firmly maintained one-party rule by the KMT, the composition of the KMT changed. By 1976 Taiwanese constituted over half of the party membership, although most of the senior positions in the party were still held by mainlanders.[24]

During Chiang Ching-kuo's sixteen years as premier and president, the proportion of Taiwanese in senior KMT positions greatly increased and in 1986 Chiang chose Lee Teng-hui, a Taiwanese, as his vice president. As president from 1988 on, Lee carried the Taiwanization of the party further, so that by 1993 70 percent of the members and 57 percent of the KMT's Central Standing Committee were Taiwanese.[25] That same year a number of prominent mainlanders, feeling marginalized by the growing influence of Taiwanese, resigned from the KMT to form the New Party.

In 1994 Lee Teng-hui justified the Taiwanization of the KMT in his much-quoted interview with the Japanese correspondent Ryutaro Shiba. He said: "Thus far every regime that has held political power in Taiwan is an alien regime. . . . Even the KMT is an alien regime. It is only a political party that came to Taiwan to rule the Taiwanese. So we must turn it into a Taiwanese KMT."[26]

The PRC watched with deep concern the growing strength of the DPP and the Taiwanization of the KMT under Lee Teng-hui's leadership. Although Lee publicly endorsed reunification, his conditioning it on the democratization of China projected it into the distant future. In his inaugural speech of May 1996, although Lee rejected Taiwan independence as "unnecessary or impossible" and offered to make a journey of peace to meet with the top leadership in Beijing, he also reiterated the position that the ROC had always been a sovereign state and stressed that the two sides of the strait had been separate jurisdictions for over forty years. Lee referred to Taiwan as "our common homeland" and said that it was entering a new era in which the people as a whole, rather than any political party, would be invested with the ruling power of the nation. It must have been clear to the leaders in Beijing that the legislative and presidential elections in Taiwan had added a new dimension to the consciousness of the people there, who felt that they constituted a political entity separate from mainland China and were entitled to their own place in the international community.

Although the DPP could no longer stigmatize the KMT as a party of outsiders, it sought to portray itself as the authentic representative of the Taiwanese people, less inclined than the KMT to compromise under PRC pressure and more determined to gain international stature for Taiwan as a separate state. Locked in intense competition with the DPP for popular support in the legislative and presidential elections, Lee boosted his personal popularity by high-profile trips abroad and co-opted from the DPP the popular campaign for UN membership. He urged the people of Taiwan to stand firm against Beijing's military intimidation and warned entrepreneurs against excessive investment on the mainland.

Thus, in order to burnish the KMT's image as the true champion of the Taiwanese people, Lee tilted toward the DPP position on Taiwan's international status and its relations with mainland China. The PRC itself contributed to this shift by antagonizing the people of Taiwan with its missile firings and by refusing to resume the Koo-Wang talks, making it more difficult for Lee to take initiatives to improve cross-strait relations without giving the appearance of succumbing to PRC pressure.

National Development Conference

In December 1996 Lee Teng-hui called a National Development Conference (NDC), composed of individuals of all walks of life from both the ruling and opposition parties, to seek a consensus on constitutional reform, economic development, and cross-strait relations. As the first popularly elected president of the ROC, with only a slim majority in the Legislative Yuan, Lee needed to assess the degree of cooperation that might be expected within the KMT and from opposition parties on particular issues.

The NDC resolutions on cross-strait relations conformed closely to existing policies, although they called on the government to strengthen the mechanisms by which opposition political parties could fully participate in major policy decisions regarding relations with the China mainland.[27] NDC participants agreed that the primary consideration in cross-strait relations should be the security of Taiwan. They proposed negotiations on a peace accord "at the appropriate juncture" and negotiations on the three links "at an opportune time." They also recommended that "ROC policy toward the mainland and foreign policy should be mutually reinforcing and complementary" and that efforts be made "to facilitate the opportune moment for the leaders of both sides to meet and create a new era of cross-strait relations."

Although the resolutions urged the government to "reduce the possibility of confrontation with the mainland by establishing sound mainland policies," they reiterated the position that

> the Republic of China is a sovereign state that must actively promote foreign relations and raise its profile in international activities in its pursuit of national survival and development. Taiwan is not a part of the "People's Republic of China" and the Republic of China government opposes dealing with the cross-strait issue through the "one country, two systems" scheme.

The resolutions called for active pursuit of accession to the World Trade Organization, the World Bank, and the International Monetary Fund, with admission to the UN as a long-term objective.

The NDC resolutions on constitutional reform produced the most controversy, causing the NP delegates to walk out of the conference. The debate on these resolutions continued in the National Assembly meeting called in May 1997 to amend the constitution. Constitutional amendments could not be adopted, as in the past, by the KMT alone, for it had lost the required three-fourths majority in the March 1996 election. It had to strike deals with other parties, which proved difficult, despite the broad consensus reached in the NDC. Fistfights broke out between members of opposing parties and the speaker of the National Assembly, Frederick Chien, threatened to resign if members did not conduct themselves civilly toward each other. The political atmosphere was roiled further by two large demonstrations of over fifty thousand people calling for the resignation of Premier Lien Chan because of the government's failure to bring to justice the perpetrators of several brutal murders of prominent persons. Lien promised that he would step down after the National Assembly completed its work.

One of the most controversial NDC proposals was to reorganize and streamline the provincial government and to suspend future elections for provincial government offices. The proposal so outraged the popular KMT governor, James Soong, that he submitted his resignation. Lee Teng-hui persuaded him to stay in office, but his future remained uncertain. Supporters of the changes argued that to make Taiwan more competitive in the twenty-first century the inefficient overlap between the central and provincial governments had to be eliminated. Moreover, a political gridlock could result if popular elections brought to office a president and a governor from different parties.

The DPP had long favored the total elimination of the provincial government in order to give Taiwan the structure of an independent state and to counter those who held that Taiwan should eventually become a province of mainland China. Consequently, the proposed downsizing of the provincial government, agreed by the KMT and DPP at the NDC, appeared to Beijing as another move by Lee Teng-hui toward an independent Taiwan.

After two months of heated debate during which both the KMT and the DPP had difficulty enforcing party discipline in support of the NDC consensus, the National Assembly in July 1997 passed eleven constitutional amendments. The principal results were to strengthen the position of the president and to abolish future elections for governor and provincial assemblymen. Henceforth, the president could appoint the premier without the consent of the Legislative Yuan. The Legislative Yuan was granted the power to pass a vote of no confidence in the premier but could do so only once in a year, and the president then had the power to dissolve the Legislative Yuan and hold new elections.

The governor and the members of the provincial assembly would serve out their current terms ending in 1998; thereafter, those positions would be filled by presidential appointment. The provincial bureaucracy would be reduced in order to eliminate overlap with the central government bureaucracy. The KMT and DPP leaders agreed to defer to another session of the National Assembly in the spring of 1998 items that failed to pass, principally a KMT-sponsored proposal to require a majority, not just a plurality, to elect a president and a DPP-sponsored proposal to provide for popular referendums.

A Disastrous KMT Defeat

The DPP viewed the coming November 1997 local elections with hope, while the KMT prepared for them with trepidation, but neither predicted the scope of the stunning DPP victory and the disastrous KMT defeat. The DPP won twelve of the twenty-three mayoral and county magistrate positions and the KMT only eight. Three went to independents. The results were even worse for the KMT than these figures suggest. Aside from the thinly populated islands of Chinmen, Matsu, and Penghu and the east coast counties of Hualien and Taitung, the KMT won only three counties in the heavily populated west side of the island, the largely rural counties of Changhua, Yunlin, and Chiayi. DPP local administrators now governed 72 percent of Taiwan's population, the KMT only 22 percent.

The KMT secretary general, Wu Po-hsiung, resigned to take responsibility for the disaster, but commentators also blamed Lee Teng-hui, who had campaigned vigorously in his native place, Taipei county, for the losing KMT candidate. Newspaper editorials began to look to the "post–Lee Teng-hui era." Some voices even suggested that Lee should step down as KMT party chairman.

Commentators advanced various reasons for the KMT's debacle. Some were local. In certain places local factions, disappointed at the failure of KMT leaders to select their favored candidate, ran him against the party-nominated candidate, thus splitting the anti-DPP vote and handing the victory to the DPP. A more important cause of the defeat, however, was an island-wide disillusionment with KMT performance. Prolonged failure to apprehend the culprits in high profile murder cases gave the impression of deteriorating law and order. The KMT was also widely criticized for corruption and "money politics." The decision to downsize the provincial government, reached in collaboration with the DPP, was roundly criticized within the KMT and weakened the party's ability to line up local factions in support of KMT candidates. The squabbling within the KMT over constitutional revision damaged the image of the party and weakened popular support for Lee himself. A public opinion poll taken soon after the election showed that approval of Lee's performance had dropped from a high of 75 percent in December 1996 to 39 percent; 46 percent of those polled expressed disapproval.[28]

DPP members regarded the election results as an important step toward replacing the KMT as Taiwan's ruling party. The party chairman, Hsu Hsin-liang, however, cautioned them not to become too proud, for the results of the December 1998 elections for the Legislative Yuan and the mayors of Taipei and Kaohsiung would depend on how the two parties performed during the coming year. He warned that national elections were different from local elections and he reminded the party that in the recent local elections the DPP received only 43 percent of the total vote compared to the KMT's 42 percent, a gain for the DPP of only 1 percent over its total in the 1993 local elections.[29] To win a national election, Hsu said, the DPP must formulate economic and cross-strait policies that meet the expectations of the people.[30]

The question of unification versus independence was not a prominent issue in the campaign, but it was implicit in decisions to vote for the DPP, a party that advocated Taiwan's independence. Party spokespeople, when questioned about the DPP's adherence to Taiwan independence, insisted that the proposal to hold a plebiscite on the issue would remain in the party charter, but they responded vaguely as to what the DPP would actually do if it became the ruling party. Hsu Hsin-liang declared that the provision would be retained, but whether it would be acted upon was another matter. He likened it to the clause in the Chinese Communist Party's constitution prescribing loyalty to Marxism, which nobody followed.[31]

Hsu has been severely criticized by party members for collaborating with Lee Teng-hui and for the moderation of his attitude toward the PRC. He has said that if he were in power, he would give first priority to promoting economic relations with mainland China, including prompt negotiations with the PRC on establishment of the "three links."[32]

Chen Shui-pien, the charismatic mayor of Taipei who has been widely regarded as the DPP's strongest candidate for the presidency in the year 2000, gained increased visibility and support from his campaigning for successful DPP candidates. He said that the results of the vote demonstrated that the course of cross-strait relations would be decided by the people and that the DPP was likely to be the future negotiator with the mainland. Unlike Hsu, he opposed the establishment of the "three links" at the present time and warned businesspeople to place the interests of the nation ahead of their commercial interests. He admitted that views on cross-strait relations differed within the DPP, as well as within the KMT and the NP, and he urged the forging of a consensus among the three parties on how to proceed.[33]

The PRC was doubtless taken aback by the size of the DPP's victory. It was slow to respond, other than to restate its standard position that it reserved the right to use force to prevent Taiwan independence. Mainland specialists on Taiwan affairs, interviewed by telephone from Taiwan, acknowledged the increased political influence of the DPP as demonstrated by the election, but they noted that the DPP position on independence was becoming fuzzier and they felt that the party was becoming more realistic as the possibility of taking power increased. They called for a dialogue between mainland China and the DPP.[34]

The DPP's victory in the local elections by no means ensures that it will gain a majority in the December 1998 Legislative Yuan election. It has a reputation of being antibusiness, and it will have to convince voters that it will be more capable than the KMT of maintaining a satisfactory rate of economic growth and managing cross-strait relations. The independence issue may prove a handicap, as it was in the National Assembly election of 1991, when the public feared that the DPP might provoke a military clash with the PRC. Moreover, in the July 1997 constitutional revision, the number of seats in the Legislative Yuan was increased from 164 to 225. The DPP may have difficulty fielding enough qualified and appealing candidates to compete with the KMT for such a large number of seats. Much will depend on whether the KMT, sobered by its defeat, will be able to reduce factional infighting and mount an effectively organized campaign.

Notes

1. Samuel S. Kim, "Taiwan and the International System: The Challenge of Legitimation," in Robert Sutter and William Johnson, eds., *Taiwan in World Affairs* (Boulder, CO: Westview Press, 1994), pp. 145–184.

2. Kim, "Taiwan and the International System," p. 157.

3. Interview with Ping-cheung Loh, secretary-general of the International Cooperation and Development Fund, *Free China Review*, vol. 47, no. 4, (April 1997) 41.

4. A retired ROC diplomat said that the ROC's economic aid in 1996 amounted to about $250 million, only 0.096 percent of the GNP, below even the 0.36 percent provided by Portugal, whose per capita GNP was only $8,480 compared to Taiwan's $11,000. Bernard T. K. Joei, "Foreign Minister's African Mission," *China Post* (January 13, 1997).

5. Joei, "Foreign Minister's."

6. *China Post* (May 7, 8, 10, and 24, 1997).

7. For a discussion of the factors causing President Mandela to make this decision, see Deon Geldenhuys, "The Politics of South Africa's 'China Switch'" *Issues and Studies*, vol. 33, no. 7 (July 1997): 93–131.

8. *New York Times* (September 8, 1997).

9. *New York Times* (August 5, 1997); *China Post* (May 20, 1997).

10. *Far Eastern Economic Review* (May 15, 1997): 14.

11. *Far Eastern Economic Review* (August 28, 1997): 18.

12. *China Post* (August 8, 1997).

13. *Washington Post* (January 21, 1997).

14. For a list of the forty-seven countries without diplomatic relations with the ROC maintaining offices in Taipei and the sixty-five countries without diplomatic relations with the ROC in which the ROC maintains official or unofficial offices, see Chiu, *Chinese Yearbook*, pp. 653–670 and 671–676.

15. Chiu, *Chinese Yearbook*, gives the texts of fifty-one agreements signed during 1995 with twenty-seven countries that had no diplomatic relations with the ROC. It also contains the texts of ten agreements between the United States and the ROC concluded by the American Institute in Taiwan and the Taipei Economic and Cultural Representative Office during 1995, as well as lists of agreements concluded from 1980 to 1994.

16. Clough, *Reaching*, p. 107.

17. Jusuf Wanandi, *Southeast Asia–China Relations* (Taipei: CAPS Papers No. 13, Chinese Council of Advanced Policy Studies, December 1996), pp. 15–16.

18. Kim, *Taiwan and the International System*, pp. 164–166.

19. "Time to Clarify the One-China Principle" interview in the *Free China Review*, vol. 46, no. 3 (March 1996): 21–22.

20. *China Post* (April 24, 1997); *Far Eastern Economic Review* (May 8, 1997).

21. Gerald Chan, *China and International Organizations: Participation in Non-Governmental Organizations Since 1971* (Hong Kong: Oxford University Press, 1989), pp. 26–32.

22. Chan, *China and International Organizations*, pp. 194, 196, 198.

23. Kim, *Taiwan and the International System*, p. 160.

24. Steven J. Hood, *The KMT and the Democratization of Taiwan* (Boulder, CO: Westview Press, 1997), p. 60.

25. Hood, *The KMT*, p. 125.

26. *Tzu Li Chou Pao (Independence Weekly)* in Chinese (May 13, 1994) translated from the Japanese version in the *Asahi Shukan* (April 1994).

27. National Development Conference Secretariat, *National Development Conference Resolutions* (Taipei, January, 1997)

28. *China Post* (December 2, 1997).

29. *Shih Chieh Jih Pao (World Journal)*. <www.Sinanet.com> (November 30, 1997).

30. *Chung Kuo Shih Pao*. <www.China Times.com> (December 1, 1997).

31. *Taiwan News:20*. <www.Sinanet.com> (December 20, 1997).

32. Comments at public meeting, George Washington University, Washington, D.C. (December 9, 1997).

33. *Taiwan News:9* <www.Sinanet.com> December 8, 1997.

34. *Chung Kuo Shih Pao*, <www.China Times.com> December 1, 1997.

Chapter 6

Managing the China-Taiwan Problem

In 1997 the debate in the United States over China policy intensified. One school of thought predicted a long-term strategic confrontation between the United States and a rising, expansionist China. Others rejected the depiction of China as an aggressive power like Germany or Japan before World War II, arguing that engaging with China to bring it constructively into the world system was preferable to policies of confrontation or containment.[1]

Most Americans agreed that China presented many problems for U.S. policymakers: violations of human rights, sales of weapons to trouble-making states, trade practices unfair to American business, and so forth. Of the various differences between Washington and Beijing, however, only those concerning Taiwan presented a risk of military conflict, as dramatized by the March 1996 confrontation in the Taiwan area.

Costs of Military Conflict

Everyone recognizes that a military conflict between the PRC and Taiwan would be extremely costly to all participants. Taiwan would suffer heavy damage and loss of life. Subjugation by the PRC would devastate the economy and the Taiwanese would be subjected to military rule, probably for a number of years, to prevent the rise of a resistance movement. Taiwan's military forces would inflict severe damage and casualties on the invaders. The PRC's modernization program would be ruinously set back by the reaction of the United States, Japan, and other powers to the use of force against Taiwan. China's neighbors would respond with increased suspicion of China and acceleration of their own military build-up. The prospect for peaceful growth and economic integration of East Asia would suffer a damaging blow.[2]

The PRC could seek to avoid the harmful consequences of an all-out assault on Taiwan by lesser military actions, ranging from an escalating series of missile firings and military exercises to imposition of a partial or complete blockade. The objective would be to force the Taiwan authorities to negotiate an agreement on unification on Beijing's terms. Such a strategy would have several drawbacks: (a) If Taiwan stood firm against escalating threats, Beijing would either fail in its objective or, if its military action were upgraded to a blockade, would be forced into an expanding conflict by Taiwan's efforts to break the blockade; (b) escalating the use of force would probably cause the United States to declare void the August 1982 communiqué on limiting the supply of arms to Taiwan, because the PRC no longer adhered to its commitment to a policy of peaceful unification; or (c) at some point the United States might intervene militarily, making the conquest of Taiwan impossible.

An escalating series of military threats or actual conflict in the Taiwan Strait would pose an agonizing dilemma for the United States. To allow Taiwan to be unified by force would severely undermine confidence in the United States in Japan, South Korea, and Southeast Asia. Many Asians would conclude that China was moving toward supplanting the United States as the dominant power in East Asia. The Japanese would rapidly strengthen their military forces and might decide that they had to have nuclear weapons. Other states, having lost confidence in the determination of the United States to keep the peace in the region, would strengthen their own defenses and adjust to China's new power position.

However, if the United States intervened militarily to prevent the forceful unification of Taiwan with mainland China, many American lives would be lost. The United States and the PRC would be caught up in another prolonged period of hostility toward each other. Washington would probably recognize Taiwan as an independent state and would be committed indefinitely to its protection. Most mainland Chinese would see the U.S. action as another infringement on China's sovereignty and would continue to regard Taiwan as *terra irredenta*. The United States, the PRC, and Taiwan would all have lost the opportunity to benefit from a peaceful, rapidly growing, increasingly interdependent East Asia. Instead, military preparedness would take precedence and consume large amounts of resources.

Why Risk Military Conflict?

If the decision makers in the PRC and Taiwan recognize the high costs of military conflict, why do they pursue policies that could lead to such a catastrophe? Obviously, both sides prefer a peaceful resolution of the Taiwan issue. But the differences between them on the status of Taiwan are so wide and are based on such strongly held convictions on both sides that little progress has been made in narrowing them.

It is an article of faith for all leaders in Beijing that Taiwan is part of China to be brought under the sovereign rule of the PRC. They may differ among themselves as to precisely how and when Taiwan should be reunified with the motherland, but there is no disagreement with that objective. Taiwan was wrested from China by a foreign power and one of the Chinese Communist Party's chief goals has been to recover this piece of Chinese territory. Since the reunification of Taiwan is a matter of China's sovereignty and territorial integrity, leaders can readily whip up nationalistic enthusiasm on the issue, particularly if reunification can be convincingly portrayed as being prevented by a foreign power. There may be a temptation to do so in order to distract public attention from the government's failure to deal effectively with difficult domestic problems.

Beijing's leaders also have important strategic reasons for wanting control of Taiwan, as discussed in Chapter 2. Joined with the mainland, Taiwan would add significantly to the PRC's economic and military power; separated, it could be used by the U.S.-Japan alliance to repress the growth of Chinese power.

So long as PRC leaders were satisfied that Taiwan would not seek global recognition as a separate, sovereign state, they could tolerate a prolonged process of unification. The two economies were becoming increasingly interdependent and other forms of interaction between the two societies steadily increased. But Lee Teng-hui seemed determined to gain recognition for Taiwan as an independent state. His pragmatic diplomacy, the bid for membership in the UN, and his trip to Cornell all seemed to be steps in that direction.

The United States continued to sell advanced weapons to Taiwan and adjusted its relationship closer to an official level. Members of Congress voted almost unanimously in favor of Lee's visit to Cornell, and individual members advocated U.S. support for Taiwan's membership in the UN. Even France was persuaded to send a cabinet minister to visit Taiwan and sold the island Mirage aircraft and frigates.

Thus, although the PRC successfully held the line against the expansion of the ROC's diplomatic relations, it was unable to prevent Taiwan from substantially improving its defense capabilities and drawing closer to official relations with important countries. Instead of responding positively to Jiang's eight-point overture of January 1995, Lee defied the PRC by his Cornell visit. PRC leaders decided that a serious warning had to be sent to Taiwan and the United States. Hence, the harsh rhetoric and military exercises.

There is no evidence that the Beijing authorities expected the missile firings and military exercises to provoke an actual clash of arms with either Taiwan or the United States. The actions were announced in advance and restricted to well-defined areas. Yet they were deliberately made more threatening than any in the recent past in order to send a strong message that the PRC could not tolerate an independent Taiwan.

The consensus in Taiwan that the island has the right to function independently in the international system is as firm as the consensus on the mainland that Taiwan should accept the status of being a subordinate part of the PRC. Public opinion polls in Taiwan consistently show that the great majority favor Taiwan's present de facto independent status rather than risking either Beijing's preferred "one country, two systems" arrangement or a military conflict with the PRC that could be triggered by a formal declaration of independence.

The question for the people of Taiwan is how far the government can go in improving the island's international status without causing the leaders in Beijing to decide that the PRC must resort to force to prevent Taiwan from achieving general recognition as an independent state. Judgments of the risk involved in particular actions to expand Taiwan's international relations depend in part on assumptions of the extent to which the PRC might be deterred from the use of force by its perception of possible U.S. responses.

Public opinion in Taiwan has been strongly in favor of actions to improve Taiwan's international status, even during the period when the PRC was firing missiles to warn against going too far in this direction. Public opinion polls commissioned by the Mainland Affairs Council from June 1995 to February 1997 show sizeable majorities during this period who considered developing foreign relations as either more important than developing cross-strait relations or at least equally important. A survey in February 1997 showed that 38.6 percent of the respondents regarded developing foreign relations as more important than developing cross-strait relations, 37.3 percent saw them as equally important, and only 17.9 percent considered the development of cross-strait relations as more important.[3]

Contest in the International Arena

Propagandists and the media on both sides of the Taiwan Strait portrayed the contest in the international arena as a zero-sum game. At times the rhetoric became strident. Yet the official positions of each side avoided challenging the other side's bottom line. The government in Taipei rejected de jure independence for Taiwan and pledged its commitment to the eventual unification of a divided China. The government in Beijing conceded Taiwan broad scope to function independently in the international community, so long as its relationships were unofficial.

The problem for the PRC has been that Taiwan *acted* like an independent state, continually seeking to expand its scope for international activity and trying to increase the officiality of its international relationships. Where should Beijing draw the line? PRC officials asserted that if Taiwan is given an inch, it will take a mile. The problem for Taiwan was the impossibility of conducting its extensive economic and other international relationships at a purely unofficial level and the need to respond to the public demand that its leaders seek greater dignity and respect from the international community.

A vigorous struggle continued along the fuzzy line between official and unofficial, even extending at times to INGOs that were by definition unofficial. The contest involved third parties. It was very complex, because broad differences often existed between politically influential groups in the target countries as to how far to go in granting Taiwan scope for activity. The position taken by politicians on the PRC/Taiwan competition could become a domestic political issue, notably in the United States, which is the most important target country.

Often the clash occurred in the realm of symbolism rather than substance. A Lee Teng-hui visit had only a minor effect on the substance of economic, cultural, and other relations between Taiwan and the country visited, but the Taiwan media trumpeted the visit as a great victory over the PRC and it was seen by the PRC as a dangerous move toward global recognition of Taiwan as an independent state. The designation of a Taiwan office abroad as an office of "the Republic of China" did not significantly improve Taiwan's substantive relations with the country concerned but was seen by the foreign ministries in Taipei and Beijing as victory or defeat in the continuing battle in the international arena.

Paradoxically, the PRC's unrelenting campaign to prevent the use of the term "Republic of China" encouraged the rest of the world to think of the island of Taiwan as a separate state called "Taiwan," which functioned independently in the world community and had never been a part of the PRC. The Taipei authorities persisted in using "Republic of China" as evidence that they considered Taiwan a part of historical China that would eventually be unified again with the rest of China.

By persuading most of the world and then many of the world-conscious Taiwan residents that the Republic of China is a defunct concept, [the PRC] only serves to whip up a separate Taiwan identity in opposition to China. . . . By winning the legitimacy contest Peking is forcing Taiwan to quit the game and find a new identity.[4]

The PRC's refusal to acknowledge the reality of "one country, two governments," both styling themselves as part of China, strengthened the political influence of those in Taiwan who would abandon the use of "Republic of China" in favor of "Republic of Taiwan."

Can the two governments moderate the intensity of the conflict over the central issue: Taiwan's status in the international arena? The PRC, as the larger and stronger contestant, is in the best position to do so. It is clearly winning the contest at the level of diplomatic relations. Its leaders should be confident that time is working in their favor. They can afford to make the small concessions needed to persuade the people of Taiwan that they will not be denied a reasonable amount of international living space. They do not need to squeeze so hard as to deny scholars in Taiwan the right to participate in CSCAP simply because it discusses security issues. Their recent success in downgrading international attendance at the Panama conference because of Lee's presence should bolster their confidence, but it remains to be seen whether that might lead them to slacken their effort to isolate Taiwan; it might only encourage them to redouble their effort.

Unless there is some evidence that the PRC is willing to ease its pressure, Taiwan's leaders will see no opportunity for moderating their own activity. From their viewpoint, maximizing the scope for Taiwan's international activities is crucial to avoiding ultimately being swallowed up by Beijing. Most people in Taiwan have accepted Lee's view that pragmatic diplomacy is essential to the survival of Taiwan as an independent international actor. Consequently, few politicians favor moderating this activity.

If moderation of the international conflict is difficult or impossible, could it continue as it did from 1979 to 1995 without causing an explosive confrontation? In other words, could the authorities on both sides of the strait promote economic and other forms of cross-strait integration without linking such behavior to trends in the international contest? In 1995 the PRC suspended the Wang-Koo talks on the grounds that the Lee visit had poisoned the cross-strait atmosphere. ROC officials frequently cite the PRC's efforts to isolate Taiwan as justification for slowing economic integration.

Economic complementarity favors the PRC, resulting in pressure on the government by Taiwan's business circles to ease restrictions on trade, investment, and direct travel and shipping. Military threats aimed at checking pragmatic diplomacy have a depressing effect on cross-strait relations. Could not the PRC sufficiently limit the ROC's international activities, as it did before June 1995, without feeling called upon to fire missiles in the Taiwan Strait? In the long run, it will be the PRC's ability to encourage closer cooperation between the people of the mainland and Taiwan that will improve prospects for unification, rather than the extent to which the PRC succeeds in circumscribing the ROC's international relations.

The Struggle Over Economic Integration

Both sides of the strait continued to benefit economically from the growth of trade and investment across the strait during 1996 and 1997. PRC officials pressed for further action on the "three links" and criticized the ROC government's "avoid haste, be patient" policy toward investments on the mainland. In Taiwan the debate between businesspeople and the government over cross-strait economic relations became more heated. As indicated in Chapter 4, the government combined certain actions to ease trade and investment restrictions with efforts to limit investment on the mainland. It sought to soften businesspeople's criticism of the go-slow policy by pointing out that only a few large enterprises were affected by the policy and that Taiwan investment in the mainland continued to grow.[5] Nevertheless, businesspeople continued to complain that the government's policy was damaging Taiwan's economy.[6]

In late 1997 cross-strait business meetings became more lively than they had been since September 1996. In November 1997 a high-level twenty-five-person delegation, headed by the chairman of Taiwan's Chamber of Commerce and Industry and including top executives in trade, shipping, electronics, engineering, chemicals, and services, visited Beijing.[7] During the same month thirty businesspeople from the mainland took part in the 24th International Business Congress, held in Taipei and attended by 1,000 representatives from sixty countries.[8] Also in November 1997 bankers in Shanghai hosted the fourth cross-strait monetary seminar, attended by 250 banking, trust, and stock professionals from both sides of the strait.[9] The following month the PRC sent a seventeen-person delegation to Taiwan, headed by the deputy director of the China Council for the Promotion of International Trade.[10]

In the debate over mainland investment, the ROC government was on the defensive. Officials advanced the customary arguments that the PRC's refusal to recognize the ROC as a political entity, to renounce the use of force, and to stop isolating Taiwan internationally should cause businesspeople to be cautious about investing in the mainland. The implication was that pressure to slow Taiwan investment might persuade Beijing to make concessions on these political issues. Beijing was disinclined to do so, however, because of its confidence in the seemingly inexorable economic trends and the rising business pressure on the Taiwan government.

The conflicting views of Lee Teng-hui and Chang Yung-fa, chairman of the Evergreen Group, illustrate the sharpening debate in Taiwan between the government and business circles over cross-strait relations. In an address to business leaders in November 1997, Lee placed greatest emphasis on resisting Beijing's efforts to isolate the ROC in the international community. He stressed the need to break out of PRC-imposed isolation in order to achieve the ROC's rightful international status and dignity. We must "shatter this fictitious international system" in which "the ROC is regarded as nonexistent," Lee declared.[11] Deeply concerned with the contest with the PRC in the international arena, Lee was disinclined to respond positively to PRC appeals and the urging of business leaders to allow more rapid integration of the two economies. Lee said that the time was not ripe to institute the "three links."

Chang Yung-fa, on the other hand, represented the most activist of business leaders who were seeking closer economic ties with the mainland. As the owner of the giant Evergreen Shipping Line and Eva Airline, with sizeable investments on the mainland, Chang has a personal stake in the early establishment of the "three links." In an interview with the *China Times* on his return from a visit to Beijing in October 1997, Chang complained that failure to establish the "three links" was very costly to the people of Taiwan. He urged the government to enter into negotiations with the PRC by sending a secret emissary. The time was right for negotiations, he said; delay would only leave Taiwan in a worse position. The issues of unification and Taiwan's scope for the exercise of sovereignty could be discussed over a lengthy period of time. Had not Deng Xiaoping himself declared, "If unification does not take place in one hundred years, it will in a thousand"? Chang said that while negotiations were going on, Taiwan's security would be protected and a better cross-strait atmosphere would be created. He revealed that he had made recommendations to Lee Teng-hui, but to no effect; he "couldn't fathom what Lee was thinking."[12]

The PRC, while pressing for political talks with Taiwan, as discussed later in this chapter, launched a drive to expand people-to-people relations across the strait. In April 1998, Qian Qichen, a politburo member and a vice premier, made an inspection trip to Shanghai and Jiangsu, where he urged further efforts to promote cross-strait economic, scientific, technological, and cultural exchanges. Qian visited a dozen Taiwan-invested enterprises in the Pudong district, listened to the views of Taiwan businesspeople, and assured them that the PRC would earnestly protect all their legitimate interests and rights. He instructed the localities and departments concerned to improve the climate for Taiwan investment.[13]

Also in April 1998, the Ministry of Foreign Trade and Economic Cooperation (MOFTEC) sponsored an important meeting in Xiamen, attended by economic and trade officials from fifteen provinces and cities, to discuss ways of expanding economic relations with Taiwan. An Min, deputy MOFTEC minister, said that "earnest measures should be taken to raise to a new level the work to increase exports to Taiwan and attract more investments from Taiwan."[14]

Prospects for Dialogue

Those persons, including U.S. officials, interested in the betterment of relations between Beijing and Taipei, frequently urged the initiation or resumption of dialogue between the two sides of the strait. What they meant by dialogue was not always clear. Dialogues could take place at three levels: between the two leaders, between lower-level government officials, or through the quasi-official SEF-ARATS channel.

The SEF-ARATS Channel

In spite of the suspension of the regular meetings of SEF and ARATS officials that had been agreed upon in 1993, these organizations continued to perform their functions of facilitating the resolution of practical people-to-people problems. As mentioned earlier, they carried out the repatriation of illegal immigrants into Taiwan, they resumed the repatriation of criminal suspects, and they agreed on the return of hijackers. Moreover, SEF and ARATS officials from time to time made visits to the other side of the strait. During April 1997 a delegation of notaries made a ten-day visit to five cities in the PRC to discuss problems that had arisen in the authentication of documents by SEF, in accordance with the agreement signed at the Singapore Koo-Wang meeting in 1993. Officials from SEF and the MAC accompanied the delegation.[15] Also in April 1997, Lee Ching-ping, deputy secretary-general of SEF, traveled to Beijing, where he met with Tang Shubei and discussed the possible resumption of regular SEF-ARATS talks. Lee also accompanied a postal delegation on a two-week visit to postal authorities in

several cities during November 1997. In July Zhang Zongxu, the mayor
of Xiamen, who had been invited by SEF in October 1995 to visit Taiwan, finally arrived, heading a delegation of businesspeople, including
the head of the ARATS economic department.[16] In August 1997 the
ARATS deputy secretary-general, Liu Gangqi, attended a seminar in
Taiwan.

Both sides in public statements advocated the resumption of regular
SEF-ARATS talks, but Taipei wanted them resumed without conditions, while Beijing insisted on prior agreement on political talks or
some form of reaffirmation by Taipei of its commitment to the one
China principle. Tang Shubei had told members of Taichung's city
council in August 1996 that it would be useless to restart the SEF-
ARATS talks under the conditions in which they had been held; they
might go on for five or ten years without producing substantial results.[17] PRC spokespeople repeatedly urged Taipei to enter into political talks in order to end the state of hostility between the two sides, as
Jiang Zemin had proposed in his "eight points." "If no efforts were
made to face political differences and strive to seek solutions, it will
be difficult to achieve successful results in working-level [SEF-ARATS]
consultations."[18] Beijing was willing, however, to employ the SEF-
ARATS channel to work out the procedures for the political talks.

In early December 1997 Lee Teng-hui appealed for the unconditional
reopening of the SEF-ARATS channel. "We want the two sides to resume as quickly as posible negotiations from where they were halted."
The PRC's Foreign Ministry spokesman promptly responded with the
standard PRC position, calling on Taipei to "come back to the principle
of 'one China' . . . and react as soon as possible to the call by Jiang
Zemin for political talks between the two sides." He then repeated the
position taken in Jiang's eight points: that "as a first step, the two sides
can, on the principle of one China, end hostilities across the strait."

Although PRC leaders opposed the resumption of formal Koo-Wang
talks before political talks had been agreed upon, they did express approval of the ongoing work of SEF and ARATS in resolving practical
problems. A lengthy September 1997 broadcast from Beijing gave a detailed report on people-to-people activities facilitated by SEF and
ARATS, pointing out that "the channels for handling routine matters
in the exchange between compatriots on the two sides of the strait have
remained unimpeded."[19] An article in the September issue of the
ARATS journal, *Cross-Strait Relations*, citing the repatriation of hijackers and other criminal suspects and the resolution of fisheries disputes,
said that "a new way of thinking" had emerged: Many routine issues
could be resolved first by a pragmatic approach, and talks to regulate
the practice could be held later, when conditions became ripe. The arti-

cle acknowledged that issues of "jurisdiction" and other sensitive political issues arose in connection with discussions aimed at resolving routine matters but urged that these be put aside and left for later political negotiations to resolve.[20]

In November 1997 an abortive attempt to bring together high-level SEF and ARATS officials occurred. ARATS invited Chiao Jen-ho, SEF's secretary-general, to lead a delegation to an early December symposium in Xiamen on prospects for cross-strait economic relations. Business people and scholars from both sides were invited, including several members of SEF's board of directors. ARATS officials indicated that the symposium would not only serve to increase understanding between economic figures on the two sides but would also provide an occasion for exchanges between SEF and ARATS. Taipei, perceiving the symposium to be an attempt to undercut its "avoid haste, be patient" policy, declined the invitation from Chiao and countered with a proposal that Koo Chen-fu lead a delegation to Beijing in mid-December. ARATS officials did not respond to this proposal and postponed the symposium, charging that it had been "politicized" by Taipei.[21] Tang Shubei reportedly told a visiting Taiwan delegation that Chiao Jen-ho should visit the PRC first, in order to reach agreement on the nature, time, location, and agenda of a meeting before Koo Chen-fu visited the mainland.[22]

Political Negotiations

Although the ROC authorities called again and again for the resumption of regular SEF-ARATS talks, they did not reject the idea of political talks. In December 1996, for example, Koo Chen-fu, the chairman of SEF, urged ARATS to agree to preparatory talks through existing negotiation channels on ways to end the hostility between the two sides and to begin an exchange of visits between the two leaders. An ARATS official told a Taipei reporter that the message had been referred to senior officials for study and added: "We would like to consult with SEF on the agenda, venue and delegates for cross-strait political talks when the time is ripe." In his September 3, 1997, press conference, Chang Ching-yu said that the MAC was studying the initiation of "policy or political dialogues" with the mainland that "would be open to a full spectrum of ideas."[23]

One key official in Taipei, however, viewed the prospect for political talks pessimistically. Chiao Jen-ho, secretary-general of SEF, told a Hong Kong *Ta Kung Pao* reporter in September 1997 that the people of Taiwan would firmly oppose such talks, because up to now thay had only considered acceptable talks on specific issues. Political talks, he thought, would last a long time, entail strenuous efforts, and would be damaging to cross-strait relations if they failed.[24]

Political talks undoubtedly will be difficult and probably lengthy. Even to get them started requires agreement on fuzzing the status of Taiwan, since neither side will accept the other's definition. But each has floated trial balloons, indicating serious search for a formula that would permit a dialogue to begin. For example, in June 1997 Wang Daohan, chairman of ARATS, while stressing the need to accept the one China principle, put forward a novel formulation: "Sovereignty cannot be cut apart, but can be shared."[25] The following month Taipei's MAC advanced a formula that also included the idea of shared sovereignty: "Shared sovereignty, divided jurisdictions." (*zhu quan gong xiang, zhi quan fen shu*). Taipei sources quoted Jiang Zemin and Qian Qichen as saying that the two sides were in "separate situations" and referred to internal documents of the PRC State Council's Taiwan Affairs Office as describing cross-strait relations as "integrated sovereignty, divided jurisdiction."[26] SEF Chairman Koo Chen-fu, on September 19 said that both sides must understand the reality of China's current political status as "shared sovereignty with separate jurisdiction." He added that recognition of China's rule by two political entities does not conflict with the "one China" principle.[27]

Wang reportedly modified still further his position on "one China" in a November 1997 statement to Hsu Li-nung, chairman of the delegation whose meeting with Tang Shubei was referred to previously. Wang said that "one China" stands for neither the PRC nor the ROC, but a unified China created by the Chinese people on both sides of the strait.[28] If the PRC were to officially adopt this position, it would be close to the ROC's formulation. However, an unidentified official in Beijing told a Hong Kong *Wen Wei Po* reporter that reports of Wang's interview were inaccurate; the PRC is the sole legitimate government of China and Taiwan is part of the PRC.[29] Officials in Taipei expressed interest in Wang's reported statement but did not consider it reliable unless officially confirmed.

The PRC's insistence on opening political talks before resuming regular meetings through the SEF-ARATS channel seemed, to an outside observer, to be placing the cart before the horse. Political conditions in Taiwan made it exceedingly difficult for the government to appear to make significant concessions to the PRC. The KMT and the DPP were engaged in a crucial struggle to gain the upper hand in the December 1998 Legislative Yuan election and the March 2000 presidential election. Both parties were beset with internal conflicts. The popularity of Lee Teng-hui and Vice President Lien Chan, Lee's putative selection for his successor in 2000, dropped to a low point in December 1997, while the popularity of Governor James Soong, whose position was scheduled to be abolished in December 1998, soared, both in public opinion polls and as reflected in his winning the most votes in the election of the KMT's Central Committee. Factional strife increased during the selection of candidates for the December elections of the Legislative Yuan and the mayors of Taipei and Kaohsiung. In the DPP the former party chairman, Hsu Hsin-liang, the mayor of Taipei, Chen Shui-pien, and the new party chairman, Lin Yi-hsiung, elected in May 1998, maneuvered warily in preparation for the presidential election in the year 2000.

Not only did Jiang Zemin seem to be in a stronger position than Lee Teng-hui to take an initiative in cross-strait relations, but resuming regular SEF-ARATS meetings would accord with the PRC's basic strategy of building cross-strait links. The channel could be used both for its original purpose of resolving practical problems in people-to-people relations and also to negotiate the conditions for opening political talks. It would seem to be in the PRC's own interest to take initiatives to strengthen cross-strait ties, rather than to hold back, bargaining for political concessions that Taipei would find difficult to give.

Although political constraints hampered a positive response by Taiwan leaders to the trial balloons appearing on the China mainland, influential individuals in addition to Chang Yung-fa stressed the need for action by the Taiwan side to help open dialogue. For example, Yu Chi-chung, publisher of a leading newspaper, *China Times*, and a member of the KMT Central Committee and of the National Unification Council, urged action at the December 1997 Council meeting.

> The time has come to remove the impasse. If we don't act, the opportunity will soon be lost. . . . If we fail to handle it properly, and if both public opinion and the military establishment across the Strait conclude that reconciliation is a lost cause and favor a hard line, it will be the greatest misfortune for the people on both sides of the Taiwan Strait.

Yu referred approvingly to a proposal made by five well-known professors, including Ma Ying-chiu, former minister of justice, to establish a joint body (*lian he hui*) composed of officials on both sides of the strait to discuss common issues at an official level. "The sooner we take some initiative, the better it will work out for us," Ma said.[30]

Despite the repetition from time to time of irreconcilable positions, the numerous appeals in the latter half of 1997 by authoritative figures on both sides for cross-strait political talks and the effort to find mutually acceptable language to describe the China mainland-Taiwan relationship suggest that both parties have been giving serious consider-

ation to actually engaging in talks on political issues, such as ending
the state of hostility between the two sides. PRC authorities have made
clear that talks would be conducted on an equal footing, not as if between a central government and a province. The task of setting aside
intractable issues and finding areas of agreement presents formidable
problems, but the concept of "shared sovereignty" might offer a se-
mantic key to resolving the difficulties.

In March 1998 SEF and ARATS drew closer to reopening the dialogue. A letter from ARATS to SEF on February 24 proposed meeting
to discuss procedural matters leading to political talks, to be followed
by arrangements for resuming talks on economic and routine issues.
The letter also welcomed a visit by Koo Chen-fu at an appropriate time,
to be arranged by exchanges of visits between ARATS and SEF personnel. Finally, after a further exchange of messages, SEF's deputy secretary-general, Jan Jyh-horng (Zhan Zhi-hong), went to Beijing to meet
with his ARATS counterpart, Li Ya-fei, thus resuming the formal SEF-
ARATS meetings that had been suspended in 1995. The two sides
agreed that Koo Chen-foo would visit the PRC during 1998.[31]

Summit Meeting

A meeting of the two leaders is unlikely. Lee has not taken any steps
to conciliate the PRC leadership. On the contrary, during his trip to
Central and South America, Lee castigated Communist China in terms
so harsh that his critics at home accused him of jeopardizing Taiwan's
interests. "Don't be scared by the size of Communist China," Lee declared. "What's the use of being big, [China] is just stupid."[32] Moreover, many officials and other observers in the PRC have expressed
grave doubts that negotiations with Lee could be fruitful. His November 1997 interviews with *Washington Post* and London *Times* reporters,
in which he referred several times to Taiwan as "an independent sovereign country," probably strengthened suspicions in Beijing that Lee's
goal is de jure independence for Taiwan, despite Foreign Minister
Jason Hu's prompt denial that Lee had said anything new.[33] A summit
meeting would require not only an improvement in the cross-strait atmosphere and a decline in Beijing's mistrust of Lee but also a lengthy,
careful period of preparation if it were to have any prospect of positive
results.

Reinvigorated PRC Campaign on the Taiwan Issue

In May 1998 the PRC held a large-scale, three-day work conference on
policy toward Taiwan, the first such conference since 1990. Attended

by most members of the politburo, with speeches by Jiang Zemin and Vice Premier Qian Qichen, it was clearly an important meeting, intended to reinvigorate activities aimed at Taiwan and to speed up progress toward unification. The leadership launched a two-pronged campaign, one directed toward increasing all forms of interaction between the people of Taiwan and the people of mainland China, the other aimed at bringing about political talks with the Taiwan authorities to produce an agreement on ending the state of hostilities between the two sides. PRC leaders instructed all government and party officials concerned with Taiwan, at the central, provincial, and local levels, to redouble their efforts to create conditions favorable for unification.

The instructions ordered officials to acquire a deep understanding of the feelings of the people of Taiwan, thoroughly take care of and respect their interests and desires, simplify entry procedures for people from Taiwan, and facilitate their travel, visits to relatives, conduct of trade, and pursuit of education.[34]

Shortly after publication of the directive, Vice Premier Qian Qichen received a delegation invited by ARATS, headed by a New Party leader, Lee Ching-hua. The purpose of the visit was to convey the views of Taiwan businesspeople concerning the regulations being drawn up to implement the law for protection of Taiwan investments. Qian assured the delegation that the PRC would earnestly study their views and do well the work of protecting the rights and interests of Taiwan businesspeople.[35]

Although the directive was mainly positive in tone, urging the improvement of relations between Taiwan and mainland China, it also called for pursuing an intense and complicated struggle against "Taiwan separatists and international anti-China forces" in order to defend the one China principle.

Possibilities for Cooperation

The opening of a dialogue would, initially, ease cross-strait tension. Over the longer term, however, dialogue would not be fruitful unless each side were willing to take steps that increased cooperation and diminished confrontation. In order to overcome deep mutual mistrust, each side needs to convince the other that its first priority is to strengthen cross-strait relations in a manner beneficial to both parties. Thus, the PRC would have to accept the view that it is not in its interest to try to bludgeon the government and people of Taiwan into a cooperative attitude by military threats and international isolation. The ROC would have to accept the view that the security and prosperity of the people of Taiwan can only be assured in the long run by developing a close and cooperative relationship with mainland China, not by strengthening military defenses and boosting Taiwan's status in the international community. Of course, neither side could be expected to give up the policies disliked by the other, but as greater emphasis on cooperation bore fruit, the perception of a need to rely on the policies disliked by the other side would gradually diminish.

Whether the two sides can bring about a gradual increase in cooperation and a decline in confrontation will depend on the shifting balance of political forces in mainland China and Taiwan. On the mainland, persons inclined toward cooperation include those benefitting from Taiwan's trade and investment—businesspeople, workers in Taiwan-invested enterprises, and local officials, particularly those in coastal China. So long as PRC leaders give a high priority to China's economic modernization, an influential cohort of central government economic officials and think-tank analysts also will favor economic cooperation with Taiwan. Even those senior officials whose greatest concern is checking Taiwan's drift toward independence recognize the importance of economic ties as instrumental to this policy. Thus, the mainstream in the PRC in late 1987 and early 1998 saw important advantages in promoting economic cooperation with Taiwan. Few, if any, criticized this policy, although many criticized the Taiwan government for not establishing the three links and in other ways moving more quickly to expand economic relations.

Commentators frequently identify the Chinese military as supporters of a hard line on Taiwan, favoring confrontation over cooperation. Certainly, the missile firings and military exercises of 1995–1996 had an adverse effect on economic cooperation across the strait. There may be military leaders who see no hope for peaceful unification, and the military have been given the mission of preparing for the use of force against Taiwan if peaceful means fail. Yet the military are more acutely aware than others of the potential high costs of the use of force. They recognize the risk that the United States might intervene, and they know better than do civilian officials of PLA military weaknesses in a confrontation with U.S. forces. Hence, PLA leaders have no reason to oppose economic and other forms of cooperation with Taiwan, with the ultimate goal of peaceful unification, even though some may be skeptical of its prospects.

Aside from those favoring economic cooperation, many others on the mainland have personal stakes in other forms of cooperation: academic, scientific, technological, journalistic, sports, performing arts, religious, tourism, suppression of crime, and so forth. Benefiting from interaction with their Taiwan counterparts, persons involved in these activities much prefer cooperation over confrontation.

On the PRC side, therefore, no significant, well-defined group opposes cross-strait cooperation with Taiwan. Only when the leaders become convinced, as they were in 1995, that Taiwan, as well as the United States, need to be sharply warned against moves toward independence does the PRC give priority to cross-strait confrontation over cooperation.

In the international community, however, confrontation is the rule for the PRC and cooperation the exception. There is only a tiny constituency on the mainland that has a personal stake in cooperation with Taiwan in the international arena. This would include, for example, those who see advantages in cooperating with counterparts from Taiwan in INGOs. The Foreign Ministry has the primary responsibility for monitoring the international actions of Taiwan and countering its efforts to enhance its international image. Given Beijing's control over the media, it is not difficult to mobilize popular opposition on nationalistic grounds to any action by Taiwan portrayed as attempting to create "two Chinas" or "one China, one Taiwan," thus obstructing reunification.

In Taiwan the political scene is far more complex. Business circles and the planning technocrats in the government, who see Taiwan's economic future as being dependent on close cooperation with the mainland, have pressed for the establishment of the three links and an easing of restrictions on trade and investment in the mainland.[36] Lee Teng-hui and other senior KMT political figures fear that economic overdependence on the mainland would enable Beijing to put political pressure on Taiwan. They would delay the three links and slow investment on the mainland. The DPP is deeply divided. Former chairman Hsu Hsin-liang, who stepped down in May 1998, has urged prompt negotiations on the three links and easing of economic restrictions. His close aide, Kuo Cheng-liang (Julian Kuo), director of the DPP Policy Council, published a lengthy critique of Lee's "go slow" policy as being tactically ineffective and strategically unwise.[37] Many of their colleagues, however, opposed these views and would be much more cautious in promoting economic cooperation with the mainland. Some would place more emphasis on improving Taiwan's international status than on economic cooperation with the PRC.

Cross-Strait Travel

Both governments recognize that visits to the other side of the strait are crucial to expanded economic interaction and enhanced mutual understanding. Most such travel, however, is on individual initiative, not arranged by governments. PRC officials impose few restrictions on individual travel from Taiwan, but they have at times disapproved exchanges proposed by the Taiwan side. MAC officials said that between 1991 and 1997 seventy-six "boycotts" of exchanges by the PRC had occurred.[38] The ROC severely restricts entry from the mainland, fearful of being overwhelmed by the massive population across the strait. The PRC understands Taiwan's need for restrictions, as evidenced by its willingness to accept the return of illegal immigrants into Taiwan, but protests that restrictions are too severe.

The PRC has been much less active than the ROC in sending journalists to the other side. Only about one hundred media representatives from mainland China visited Taiwan between 1991 and 1997. In April 1998, after a long hiatus, sixteen senior media officials from eleven different agencies in Beijing made a ten-day visit to Taiwan. The delegation was headed by Xie Hong, the deputy editor-in-chief of the *People's Daily*. The director of the Government Information Office in Taipei, Chen Chien-jen, said that his government would welcome long-term coverage of Taiwan affairs by mainland journalists who would reside in Taipei on a two-month rotation basis similar to that followed by Taiwan journalists covering the mainland. Adoption of this proposal by the PRC would contribute to improved understanding of Taiwan in mainland China.[39]

The ROC could take steps toward greater cooperation by further easing entry to Taiwan for business purposes. The increase in business visitors from 1,144 in 1996 to 1,287 in the first seven months of 1997 reflects a lessening of restrictions, but the number of business visitors is still small and more could be done to facilitate cross-strait economic activity.[40] The PRC could reduce or end its boycotts of proposed exchanges, permit more journalists invited by the Taiwan side to go there, and station journalists in Taiwan for long enough periods to better understand and report on developments there. The PRC could invite DPP politicians to visit the mainland. A step in that direction was an article in the December 1997 issue of the ARATS publication, *Cross-Strait Relations*, entitled "Hoping Taiwan Mayors and Magistrates Can Contribute to Cross-Strait Relations."[41] As prospects grow brighter for a takeover of power by the DPP, PRC leaders are beginning to recognize the importance of promoting greater understanding between themselves and the DPP.

Economic Interaction

It is in this area that the mutually beneficial effects of cooperation can be most readily observed. The ROC government, despite the concerns of Lee and others as to excessive dependence on the PRC, has responded to business pressures by continuing to approve small and medium-sized investments on the mainland, increasing the categories of goods that can be imported from the mainland, setting up the transshipment center in Kaohsiung, and in March 1998 authorizing cargo shipments between Shanghai and Keelung, with a brief intermediate stop at the Japanese island of Ishigaki.

The PRC has tried to improve the investment environment for Taiwan investors through its Law of the People's Republic of China on Protecting the Investment of the Compatriots of Taiwan, but investors complained of problems and during 1997 and early 1998 PRC economic officials consulted with Taiwan investors and local officials to formulate "Implementation Regulations" to remedy shortcomings in the law. Taiwan investors, however, felt disadvantaged by being unable to appeal to their own government for help when disputes arose. The negotiation of an investment guarantee agreement was on the agenda for the aborted Koo-Wang meeting of July 1995 and resumption of negotiations on this issue would be a step toward improving conditions for Taiwan investors on the China mainland.

Cooperation and Confrontation in the International Arena

The PRC has strong motivations to win the goodwill of Taiwan's business community in order to promote economic cooperation across the strait. Yet when it attempts to hinder Taiwan's official efforts to improve the investment climate for Taiwan investors in Southeast Asia (for example, Lee Teng-hui's visit to the Philippines in 1994 with a large retinue of economic officials and leading businesspeople) it creates animosity toward the PRC in Taiwan business circles. This reaction, in turn, strengthens mistrust of the PRC and support for Lee Teng-hui's policy of limiting investment on the mainland.

The financial crisis in East Asia that began in the summer of 1997 provided an opportunity for Taiwan to strengthen its ties with Southeast Asia, eliciting protests from Beijing. Taiwan weathered the crisis better than the countries of Southeast Asia and publicly offered to extend them financial help. It proposed contributing to aid mechanisms that would be administered by APEC or the ADB. The United States, however, objected to setting up a separate Asian fund, on the grounds that aid would more likely be successful if administered through only one agency, the International Monetary Fund. Another Taiwan initiative to assist Southeast Asian countries was to have its Central Bank set aside a fund of $1.22 billion to make low-interest loans to Taiwan firms to enable them to continue operating despite the high interest rates in Southeast Asia caused by the financial crisis.[42]

Frequent high-level contacts occurred between Taiwan and Southeast Asian countries to discuss the crisis. Singapore prime minister Goh Chok Tong and Malaysian prime minister Mahatir Mohamad both made transit stops in Taiwan. Vice President Lien Chan made a "vacation visit" to Singapore in January 1998 and in March visited Malaysia to consult with the premier and deputy premier on ways in which Taiwan could help stimulate economic recovery. Chiang Pin-kung, chairman of the Council for Economic Planning and Development, led a delegation of eighty prominent industrialists to Southeast Asia and Premier Vincent Siew visited the Philippines, Indonesia, and Malaysia. Beijing criticized Taiwan for using its economic muscle to promote official contacts and warned Southeast Asian countries not to accept official help from Taiwan. These warnings seemed pro forma, however, for the PRC could not use pressure on these countries to reject Taiwan's help without damaging its own relations with them.

The PRC not only has had difficulty in preventing Taiwan from enhancing its international status through economic means, it has from time to time found it advisable to participate in important international economic meetings held in Taiwan. A recent striking example was the Second APEC Technomart, an exhibit of advanced technologies provided by 501 firms from twelve APEC countries, held in Taipei in January 1998. Lin Quan, secretary-general of the PRC's State Science and Technology Commission, who headed a delegation of 220 persons, stressed the growing technological cooperation with Taiwan. Of the 1,100 items of advanced technology exhibited, the PRC furnished 403 and Taiwan 506. The exhibition demonstrated that the PRC and Taiwan could cooperate in an intergovernmental meeting considered to be of high importance to their economic progress. The PRC, however, placed a political ceiling on cross-strait cooperation by insisting that the welcoming address be made by the ROC's economics minister, rather than the deputy premier, as Taipei had planned.[43]

APEC has provided exceptional opportunities for Taiwan to participate, together with the PRC, in intergovernmental activities. Although articles on APEC in the Taiwan media tended to focus on the negative—the exclusion of Lee Teng-hui from APEC leaders' meetings—Taiwan officials up to and including the ministerial level have fully participated in a wide range of APEC activities. Bureaucrats from various government agencies, who are excluded from the United Nations and nearly all other intergovernmental organizations, have had opportunities through APEC to gain valuable experience in multilateral negotiations. During recent years, mid-level officials from both sides of the strait have taken part in APEC working group meetings in Taiwan or mainland China to discuss with other APEC members subjects such as developing small and medium-sized firms, energy, technological cooperation, and liberalizing trade in services.[44]

The PRC took part in a high-level international economic meeting in Taipei in November 1997, the conference of the International Organization of Securities Commissions to discuss the development and integration of global securities markets. Beijing sent an eleven-member delegation headed by Chen Dongzhang, vice chairman of the China Securities Regulatory Commission. All of the Group of Seven industrial countries participated. This meeting was of special importance to Beijing and Taipei, occurring while the East Asian financial crisis was unfolding.[45] The securities commissions in Taipei, Hong Kong, Shanghai, and Shenzhen work closely with each other. Early in 1998, the chairman of the Hong Kong Securities and Futures Commission, Anthony Neoh, and the chairman of the Taipei Securities Commission, Lu Daung-yen, traveled to Beijing, where they met with Zhu Rongji. Lu, who ranks just below a vice-minister, was the highest ranking Taiwan official to meet with Zhu.[46]

Taiwan's growing technological skills qualified it for admission to the Global Government Forum (GGF) in January 1998 under the name "Chinese Taipei." The GGF is primarily an industry-level body, established by the United States and Japan in 1996 to oversee the U.S.-Japan semiconductor production agreement. South Korea and the European Union subsequently joined. The organization holds one governmental meeting a year, at the level of U.S. Assistant Trade Representative (in Taiwan, the director-general of the Board of Foreign Trade of the Economics Ministry). Taiwan, as the fourth largest semiconductor producer, after the United States, Japan, and South Korea, was in a strong position to gain admission to the organization. The PRC is not a member.

A noneconomic international meeting in Taipei, to which the PRC objected but was unable to prevent, was the Asia-Pacific meeting of the International Association of Chiefs of Police, held in January 1998. Sixty senior police officers from eighteen countries took part, including the United States, Australia, Japan, Britain, Canada, the Philippines, Thailand, Malaysia, Singapore, and Brazil. The members of the organization were unwilling to allow Beijing to veto Taipei as a meeting place, even though that meant that PRC officials would not attend.[47]

Conclusions

The breadth of the difference between the PRC and the ROC concerning the status of Taiwan, which engenders an unremitting struggle in the international arena, makes its settlement very difficult. If the DPP were to come to power and reject any possibility of reunification, the prospect for a negotiated settlement would recede indefinitely and the danger of a military clash would increase sharply. In order to avoid such a crisis, leaders on both sides need to focus on areas where they can cooperate, setting aside differences as much as possible. Cooperation does not require resolution of the unification issue, but it does require avoidance of any attempt to force a solution prematurely. Differences can be tolerated, so long as cooperation is increasing.

To increase cooperation, however, requires lessening of mistrust on both sides. The people on each side of the strait need to learn to respect the feelings of the people on the other side. Those on the mainland need to understand the feelings of resistance to oppression by outsiders that exist among the people of Taiwan, generated over one hundred years of separation from the China mainland. Those in Taiwan need to understand the feelings of nationalism generated by one hundred years of humiliation by foreign powers, of pride in China's having "stood up," and of hope created by the frenzied dash toward modernization over the past twenty years.

Steady progress in cross-strait cooperation will lessen mistrust and improve prospects for eventual agreement on a special political relationship between Taiwan and mainland China, closer than that between most sovereign states. The ROC already accepts the view that "relations between the two sides of the Taiwan Strait are not those between separate countries, neither are they purely domestic in nature." The interaction of the people on the two sides of the strait is creating what Taipei political scientist Wei Yung calls "linkage communities."[48]

The process of building linkage communities and lessening mistrust between the two sides of the strait will take time. To try to rush the negotiation of a formal political relationship would be a mistake. Eventually, it should be possible to agree on a special form of association, probably one that will not fit into traditional political science or international relations categories. In the meantime, cooperation will have to be enhanced and differences managed with care.

Notes

1. *The Coming Conflict with China*, by Ross Munro and Richard Bernstein (New York: Alfred A. Knopf, 1997), was the most frequently cited example of the first view. *The Weekly Standard* (December 9, 1996; January 20, 1997; and February 24, 1997) published a series of editorials and articles critical of the Clinton administration's engagement policy toward China, written by Robert

Kagan, Gary Bauer, Christopher Cox, Jesse Helms, Martin Lee, William Trip-lett, and others. Those disagreeing with the view of China as an aggressive threat included Michael Swaine ("Don't Demonize China," *Washington Post*, [May 18, 1997]) and Robert Ross ("Beijing as a Conservative Power," *Foreign Affairs* [March–April 1997]: 33–44). Ross also coauthored, with Andrew J. Nathan, *The Great Wall and the Empty Fortress* (New York: Norton, 1997), taking issue with the depiction of China as a looming threat. James Miles, in *The Legacy of Tiananmen: China in Disarray* (Ann Arbor: University of Michigan, 1996), focuses on China's many weaknesses and sees its main threat as being from disorder rather than aggressive intent.

2. For possible scenarios of cross-strait conflict, see Martin L. Lasater, *U.S. Interests in the New Taiwan* (Boulder, CO: Westview Press, 1993, pp. 133–164), Paul H.B. Godwin, "The Use of Military Force Against Taiwan: Potential PRC Scenarios," in Parris H. Chang and Martin Lasater, eds., *If the PRC Crosses the Taiwan Strait: The International Response* (Lanham, MD: University Press of America, 1993, pp. 15–33). Also Chapter 8 in Ross Munro and Richard Bernstein, *The Coming Conflict With China*, and Cheng Lang-ping, *Yi Jiu Jiu Wu, Jun Ba Yue* (The Warning of Taiwan Strait War [Taipei: Shang Chou Wen Hua Shih Yeh, 1994]); and James R. Lilley and Chuck Downs, eds. *Crisis in the Taiwan Strait* (Washington, D.C.: National Defense University Press, 1997).

3. Mainland Affairs Council, Taipei, *Public Opinion on Cross-Strait Relations in the Republic of China, April 1997.* See also Lin Cheng-yi, "Wu Shih Wai Chiao Yu Liang An Kuan Hsi Wu Fa Bing Chung?" ("Cannot Pragmatic Diplomacy and Cross-Strait Relations Be Equally Important?") (Taipei: KMT Central Policy Committee); *Cheng Ts'e Yueh Kan* (*Policy Monthly*) no. 23, Dec. 1, 1996, pp. 15–17.

4. Wu Yu-shan, "Debate Over One China Is a Question of Identity," *Free China Journal* (August 23, 1997): 7.

5. MAC News Briefing, No. 0045, Taipei (October 20, 1997): p. 3.

6. Julian Baum, "Pushing the Envelope: Businessmen Chafe at Political Curbs on China Projects," *Far Eastern Economic Review* (October 9, 1997): 52–58.

7. *China Post* (November 11, 1997).

8. *Free China Journal* (November 21, 1997).

9. *Xinhua* (November 13, 1997, via World News Connection [*FBIS*]).

10. Taipei: *Central News Agency* (December 8, 1997).

11. *Chung Yang Jih Pao* (November 18, 1997, via World News Connection [FBIS]).

12. <www.chinatimes.com> (October 15, 1997).

13. *Xinhua*, Domestic Service in Chinese (April 19, 1998).

14. *Xinhua*, in English (April 10, 1998).

15. Hsieh Fu-yuan, "Jian Mian Gou Tong, Hao Ban Shi" ("Face-to-Face Discussions Make Work Go Well") *Chiao Liu*, no. 34, (August 1997): 30–31; *China Post* (April 30, 1997). By the end of 1996 documents sent to SEF from the mainland for authentication exceeded 190,000 and 53,000 authenticated documents had been sent to the mainland by SEF.

16. "Lin Jin Jiu Su, Cheng Yuan Ke; Zhi Lai An Tou, Chun Yi Zhi" ("Visitor Arrives from Long-Separated Neighbor; Looking Up from the Desk, Spring Buds Appear") *Chiao Liu*, no. 34, (August 1997): 19–20.

17. *China Post* (August 19, 1996).

18. *Xinhua* (October 13, 1997, via World News Connection [FBIS]).

19. Beijing: Central People's Radio (September 7, 1997, via World News Connection [FBIS]).

20. *Xinhua* (September 9, 1997, via World News Connection [FBIS]).

21. *Xinhua* (November 19, 1997; via World News Connection [FBIS]); Taiwan: *Central News Agency* (November 14, 1997, via World News Connection [FBIS]); *Free China Journal* (November 14, 1997).

22. *China Post* (November 17, 1997). The visiting delegation was headed by Hsu Li-nung, a New Party National Assembly member, but Hsu said that the trip was not organized by the New Party but by a private organization, the Chinese Alliance for Democratic Reform (*Hsin Tung Meng Hui*).

23. *MAC News Briefing*, No. 0040, Taipei (September 8, 1997).

24. *Ta Kung Pao* (September 4, 1997, via World News Connection [FBIS]).

25. *Chung Kuo Shih Pao* (June 26, 1997, via World News Connection [FBIS]).

26. *Chiao Liu* 35 (October 1997): 7; Lee Ching-ping, "End to Cross-strait Impasse Depends on Mutual Trust," *Free China Journal* (November 28, 1997). Lee is deputy secretary-general of the SEF.

27. *Free China Journal* (September 26, 1997).

28. Taipei, Central News Agency (November 17, 1997), via World News Connection [FBIS].

29. Hong Kong, *Wen Wei Po* (November 19, 1997, via World News Connection [FBIS]).

30. *Chung Kuo Shih Pao* (*China Times*) (December 7, 1997); *China Post* (December 4, 1997).

31. *Washington Post* (April 24, 1998); *Chung Yang Jih Pao* (April 24, 1998).

32. Jeffrey Parker (*Reuter*), "Lee's PRC-Bashing Risks ROC Interests," *China Post* (September 20, 1997).

33. *Washington Post* (November 8, 11, 1997); *Far Eastern Economic Review* (November 20, 1997): 31. The Office of the President issued a clarification on November 10, quoting Lee as having repeated the standard position that "the Republic of China has always been a sovereign and independent state" and rejecting "Taiwan independence" as a euphemism for establishing a new country, namely "the Republic of Taiwan." In a further clarification, the Taiwan Economic and Cultural Representative Office in Washington, D.C., explained to the *Washington Post* that Lee's meaning was that "the Republic of China is an independent and sovereign state" and not that "Taiwan is an independent and sovereign state." TECRO pointed out that in journalistic language "the Republic of China on Taiwan" and "Taiwan" were often used interchangeably, but in this case a clear distinction was needed.

34. *People's Daily.* (May 14, 1998). <www.peopledaily.com>

35. *Xinhua* (May 19,1998, via World News Connection [FBIS]).

36. Yun-han Chu, "The Political Economy of Taiwan's Mainland Policy," *Journal of Contemporary China*, vol. 6, no. 15, (July 1997): 229–258.

37. *Chung Kuo Shih Pao* (February 6, 1998).

38. *MAC News Briefing*, No. 0052, Taipei (December 8, 1997): 2; see also book-

let published by the MAC, September 1997, *Cross-Strait Exchanges: The ROC Government's Liberalization Measures and Mainland China's Blocking Attempts.*

39. *Free China Journal* (April 17, 1998); Hong Kong *Wen Wei Po* (April 15, 1998, via World News Connection [FBIS]).

40. MAC, *Beyond the Historical Gap*, Taipei, p. 369.

41. *Free China Journal* (January 16, 1998).

42. *China Post* (January 6, 1998).

43. *China Post* (January 22, 1998); *Free China Journal* (February 6, 1998).

44. Gary Klintworth, "China's Evolving Role in APEC," *International Journal*, vol. 50, no. 3 (Summer 1995): 503–506.

45. *China Post* (November 5, 1997).

46. Comments by Anthony Neoh at Hong Kong Economic and Trade Office, Washington, D.C. (April 16, 1998).

47. *China Post* (January 13, 1998).

48. Yung Wei, *From "Multi-System Nations" to "Linkage Communities: A New Conceptual Scheme for the Integration of Divided Nations.* Occasional Papers/Reprint Series in Contemporary Asian Studies, no. 1—1998 (Baltimore, MD: School of Law, University of Maryland).

Chapter 7

The Role of the United States

The governments of Beijing, Taipei, and Washington all agree that the United States has a role to play in the evolving relationship between Taiwan and mainland China, although they disagree on what that role should be. The main concern in Beijing is that the United States encourage the unification of Taiwan with mainland China under the "one country, two systems" arrangement and avoid actions favoring Taiwan independence. Taipei wants a continuing supply of arms, firm opposition to any use of force in the Taiwan Strait, and avoidance of pressure to negotiate on PRC terms. Washington sees its role as deterring the use of force by the PRC, warning Taiwan against moving toward de jure independence, and urging both parties to enter into a dialogue that could lead to an eventual peaceful settlement. The United States is inextricably involved in the dispute between Beijing and Taipei; its action or inaction will affect the way the other two parties behave.

In fashioning its role toward the Beijing-Taipei relationship, the United States must be guided by its national interests. These include peace and stability in the Asia-Pacific area, access to the economies of the region for U.S. firms and individuals, suppression of the drug trade and other criminal activity, protection of the environment, and progress in defense of human rights and democratization.[1] All of these interests would be promoted by a peaceful, constructive relationship between Taiwan and mainland China. They would be seriously jeopardized by military conflict in the Taiwan Strait.

The interests of the people of mainland China and Taiwan are very much in line with the U.S. interests outlined here. Certainly, a military conflict in the Taiwan Strait would be contrary to the interests of the peoples of these two areas, as well as to the people of the United States. The people of mainland China and Taiwan have interests, however, not shared by the American people. The Chinese in mainland China have a strong interest in unifying Taiwan with mainland China, which, under

113

certain circumstances, might be whipped up to the point where it would override their dislike of military conflict. Similarly, the people of Taiwan have a strong interest in deciding their own future, which might impel their government to actions that would risk provoking a military attack by Beijing.

The flourishing travel, trade, investment, and other forms of interaction between the peoples on either side of the Taiwan Strait have demonstrated that a close relationship between Taiwan and mainland China is inevitable and beneficial to both. The pragmatic people of Taiwan have recognized that to maintain this mutually advantageous relationship, they must take account of Beijing's views. The United States must also do so in shaping its policy, not "kowtowing" to Beijing but accepting the reality that PRC leaders have a legitimate interest in Taiwan's future. U.S. policy should encourage Beijing and Taipei to seek a middle ground, compromises that both can live with, even though neither may be fully satisfied.

Five Assumptions

The discussion of U.S. policy that follows is based on five assumptions:

1. That the PRC's economic and military power will increase, relative to that of Taiwan;
2. That the PRC will not abandon its determination to unify Taiwan with mainland China (although the form of unification is negotiable and there is no timetable);
3. That the PRC will not renounce its right to use force to prevent the establishment of Taiwan as an independent, sovereign state (although it would much prefer peaceful unification and will strive to achieve it);
4. That the people of Taiwan will continue to try to augment their freedom of action and status in the international community (although some will criticize "provocative" behavior, urge restraint, and would seek a balance in the expansion of international and cross-strait relations);
5. That the complementarity of the economies of mainland China and Taiwan will continue to exist and the economic links will continue to grow (although concern in Taiwan with overdependence on the mainland will persist).

Primary Goal and Strategy

The United States has a variety of goals with respect to the PRC and Taiwan—strategic, economic, environmental, political and others—in pursuance of the U.S. interests in the Asia-Pacific region outlined previously. The primary goal, however, on which this chapter focuses, is *to prevent the development of a crisis in the Taiwan Strait in which the United States would be compelled to choose between allowing Taiwan to be subjugated by military force or intervening with U.S. forces to prevent it.*

The proposed strategy, stated in the simplest of terms, consists of two parts: (a) encouraging the expansion of mutually beneficial cooperation of all kinds between Taiwan and mainland China, and (b) avoiding actions that increase tendencies toward confrontation between Beijing and Taipei. Policies to be followed under this strategy are spelled out in the following sections.

Reacting to Political Change in Taiwan

A primary problem for the United States in managing the Taiwan issue is the changing political scene in Taiwan. As indicated in Chapter 5, gains by the DPP in the November 1997 local elections raise the distinct possibility that it might become the ruling party by the year 2000. Encouraged by that prospect, Hsu Hsin-liang and Chen Shui-pien, possible DPP candidates for president in the year 2000, visited the United States early in 1998 in order to heighten their visibility among their countrymen and to reassure Americans that they are responsible political leaders.

Hsu and Chen reiterated the now standard DPP position that it will not be necessary to declare independence when the party takes power, because Taiwan is already an independent, sovereign state. Both favored retaining in the party charter the provision for a plebiscite on independence, but they would not necessarily activate it. Chen indicated that it could be held in reserve to deter hostile actions by the PRC. Both stressed that their highest priority was the security and prosperity of the people of Taiwan and insisted that they would not give the PRC any pretext to attack Taiwan.

The access to power in Taiwan of a party whose leaders reject the concept of eventual reunification of Taiwan with mainland China would call into question the "one China" policy that the United States has adhered to since the issuance of the Shanghai communiqué in 1972. At that time the KMT under Chiang Kai-shek was firmly committed to reunification. Hence, the United States could "acknowledge" in that communiqué "that all Chinese on either side of the Taiwan Strait maintain that there is but one China and that Taiwan is part of China" and declare that "the U.S. government does not challenge that position." At that time, this U.S. declaration coincided with the views expressed by the governments in both Beijing and Taipei.[2]

Under the leadership of Chiang Ching-kuo, the KMT continued to reiterate its commitment to reunification. And in the 1982 joint communiqué on arms sales to Taiwan, the United States assured the PRC that it had no intention of pursuing a policy of "two Chinas" or "one China, one Taiwan." In a letter dated April 5, 1982, President Ronald Reagan stated to Vice Chairman Deng Xiaoping, "There is only one China. We will not permit the unofficial relation between the American people and the people of Taiwan to weaken our commitment to that principle."[3]

When Lee Teng-hui succeeded Chiang Ching-kuo as president of the ROC and chairman of the KMT in 1988, he maintained the commitment of the government and party to reunification. In his inaugural address of May 20, 1990, Lee declared: "Taiwan and the mainland are indivisible parts of China's territory, and all Chinese are compatriots of the same flesh and blood." In the same speech he envisaged negotiations on reunification when the Chinese Communist authorities had established a democratic system and free economy, renounced the use of force against Taiwan, and stopped interfering with the ROC's foreign relations. He reiterated that the ROC was "an independent and sovereign nation."[4]

In 1990 Lee established a National Unification Council (NUC) to advise him on policy toward mainland China and in 1991 the NUC announced a set of guidelines for national unification, which were adopted by the Executive Yuan. The guidelines set out short-term, medium-term, and long-term phases leading to unification.[5] The ROC defined the cross-strait relationship as "one China, two equal political entities"; referred to the division of China into two separate governments as "a temporary, transitional phenomenon in Chinese history"; and called for joint efforts of the two sides to "put China once again on the road to unification."[6]

The reaffirmation of the "one China" policy by the KMT under Lee Teng-hui provided the basis for the United States to continue to declare its adherence to a "one China" policy.[7] In the joint statement following President Jiang Zemin's visit to Washington in October 1997, as well as the joint press conference, the United States repeated its adherence to the "one China" policy and the principles set forth in the three U.S.-China joint communiqués.[8]

Thus, the "one China" policy of the United States has continued to coincide rhetorically in a general sense with the "one China" policies of Beijing and Taipei. Of course, each of those governments defines "one China" differently; only by not attempting to define the meaning attached to "one China" has the United States been able to appear to agree in principle with both definitions. The United States has taken the further step of declaring that it does not support Taiwan independence, responding both to the PRC's long-term opposition to Taiwan independence and Lee Teng-hui's statement in his 1996 inaugural address that "it is totally unnecessary or impossible to adopt the so-called course of Taiwan independence."[9]

As prospects for gaining power brightened, DPP leaders felt a need to confront the differences among them by seeking a consensus on policy toward mainland China. Consequently, representatives of the four principal party factions debated the subject for three days in mid-February 1998. The result was agreement on a slogan, *chiang ben, xi jin* ("Strengthen the base, advance West"), which bridged (but did not resolve) the differences between those who would vigorously strengthen economic ties with the mainland and those who would only proceed slowly and cautiously. All agreed, however, that Taiwan was a de facto sovereign nation and that it would not declare itself independent. No one advocated a "one China" policy or envisaged the eventual unification of Taiwan with mainland China. This is the basic difference between the KMT and the DPP.

Chen Shui-pien did not attend the debate. During his Washington visit, however, he may have hinted at flexibility on the "one China" issue. Asked whether Taiwan was part of China, he reportedly replied: "Taiwan is not part of China if China is equivalent to the People's Republic of China," thus leaving open the possibility that Taiwan could be part of a China otherwise defined.[10]

If the DPP took power; stressed the historical, cultural, and linguistic differences between Taiwanese and mainland Chinese; sought recognition for Taiwan as an independent state; and totally rejected eventual unification with mainland China, what would become of the "one China" policy of the United States? If Taipei no longer subscribed to it, for the United States to do so would be seen as U.S. support of the PRC definition of "one China." On the other hand, U.S. abandonment of the "one China" policy would be seen in Beijing as support of Taiwan independence, convincing many that the Taiwan question could be resolved only by military means.

Resolution of the Taiwan question by peaceful means will require keeping the door open to some form of close association of Taiwan with mainland China that will satisfy Beijing's desire for unification as well as the desire of the people of Taiwan to determine their own future. As the presidential election in the year 2000 approaches, Taiwan's policy toward mainland China is likely to be a major issue. Candidates will have to satisfy voters that the policies they propose will not risk provoking a conflict with the PRC and thus strain relations with the United States. As the time for the election draws near, it will be increasingly important for the United States to reiterate its unwillingness to support Taiwan independence and its interest in growing cooperation between Taiwan and the PRC, as discussed in the following section.

Stressing Cooperation

In order to counter the widespread view in mainland China that the United States favors a separate state of Taiwan, the U.S. government should publicly state its expectation that the people of Taiwan and mainland China will develop ever closer and more cooperative relations. It is not enough to reiterate a commitment to a "one China" policy and to disavow support for Taiwan independence. U.S. officials should note and applaud evidence of growing people-to-people cooperation between Taiwan and mainland China, making clear that this trend is in the U.S. interest. Specific suggestions as to the form that political relations between the two areas might take would be unwise; that should be worked out by the two governments. But the U.S. government can and should stress the importance to the United States of the growing economic integration of Taiwan, Hong Kong, and mainland China.

The increasing economic interdependence between the two sides of the strait serves U.S. interests, not only by reducing the danger of armed conflict, but, in a positive way, by augmenting the value of the two localities as trading partners of the United States. Already, the PRC is the sixth largest U.S. trading partner and Taiwan is the eighth largest. Both are also important recipients of direct investments from U.S. firms. Many American firms operate on both sides of the strait and thus benefit from a reduction of barriers and increased cooperation between the two. When American officials, former officials, or scholars visit Taiwan, they should arrange meetings not only with officials, politicians, and scholars, but also with business leaders, such as Chang Yung-fa and Wang Yung-ching, who favor closer economic relations with mainland China.

In promoting economic interaction, the people of Taiwan and mainland China are contributing to a worldwide trend toward greater economic interdependence. The two governments are also furthering that trend by their activities in APEC and the measures that each is taking to qualify for membership in the World Trade Organization.

Taiwan has also played an important role in another global trend, the trend toward democratization. The PRC, however, has been, in President Clinton's words, "on the wrong side of history."[11] Many Americans believe that continuation of economic modernization and social change in mainland China will, in time, also impel that society toward political democracy. The people of Taiwan can have a more significant influence on that process if they are creating a close political association with mainland China rather than seeking to become a separate, independent state. Thus, U.S. interests in expanding global economic interdependence and in democratization would both be served by a Taiwan that was drawing closer to mainland China rather than pulling away.

Reiterating How U.S. Policy Has Benefited Both Sides of the Strait

In conversations with PRC, ROC, and Hong Kong officials and in presentations to the three areas, it is important to emphasize that U.S. policy over nearly twenty years has made possible remarkable achievements on both sides of the strait. Although U.S. policy has not met the desires of the two governments and could not do so, as long as their views on the status of Taiwan are so far apart, it has contributed to the striking economic and social gains made in mainland China and Taiwan, as well as to the expansion of cross-strait interaction. Anyone recommending a radical change in the policies followed by the United States since 1979 must convince U.S. decision makers that the change will not upset the highly favorable trends in and between mainland China and Taiwan.

For the people of Taiwan the past twenty years have brought increasing prosperity, democratization, growing cooperation across the Taiwan Strait, greatly expanded substantive relations with Taiwan's most important trading partners, and freedom to travel, trade, and invest abroad. All of this has been tolerable to the PRC, although falling short of hoped-for progress toward unification. The situation has not been entirely satisfactory to the people of Taiwan, either. They would like to be treated with greater respect and dignity by the international community and be allowed to take part in intergovernmental activities. Hence, they have embarked on the campaign for UN participation and have applauded visits abroad by the head of state and the premier, which appear to the PRC to be aimed toward achieving recognition for Taiwan as a de jure independent state.

The policy of the United States should be to persuade Beijing and Taipei to continue to live with a not entirely satisfactory status quo, rather than to press for an ideal solution that the other side cannot accept. The "status quo" will be dynamic rather than static, requiring continual policy adjustments, but these changes should be limited to those that the other party can tolerate.

The argument is being made, particularly by DPP spokesmen, that the United States should be prepared to underwrite democratic Taiwan as an independent, sovereign state, regardless of the PRC reaction. As Parris Chang, a DPP member of the Legislative Yuan, put it: "U.S. officials, current and former, should stop acting like China has a say in Taiwan's future."[12] Most Americans, while sympathetic with the desires of the people of Taiwan to win greater respect from the international community, would be unwilling to be drawn into a conflict with the PRC to satisfy those desires. They would ask: "Why should Americans fight, not to ensure continuation of the relatively comfortable life enjoyed by the people of Taiwan during the past twenty years, but to enable them to gain ground in the symbolic area most sensitive to the PRC?"

The United States should continue to take the middle ground, neither endorsing PRC-style unification nor underwriting de jure independence for Taiwan. Its policy should be to encourage the ongoing process of building linkage communities across the strait and continuing to oppose any use of force against Taiwan. Patience and persistence in this policy may be required for a number of years, until a decline in reciprocal mistrust makes it possible for the two sides to reach agreement on their political relationship.

Publicizing PRC-Taiwan Cooperation in Intergovernmental Agencies

As the result of considerable international pressure, the PRC agreed to Taiwan's membership in the Asian Development Bank, APEC, and (when both qualify for membership) the World Trade Organization. These organizations offer unusual opportunities for cooperation between Beijing and Taipei in the international arena, rather than the usual conflict. The United States should give special support and publicity to instances of cooperation between Taiwan and the PRC, such as the January 1998 APEC Technomart in Taipei. The United States should downplay differences over symbolic issues, such as attendance at the APEC summit, while playing up the substantive cooperation between Taipei and Beijing in APEC meetings at and below the ministerial level.

Mobilizing International Support for the U.S. Position

The principal countries with interests in East Asia—Japan, the European Union, the ASEAN states, South Korea, Australia and Canada—

would look favorably on a U.S. strategy toward mainland China and Taiwan such as that outlined previously. All have adopted some form of one China policy and do not support formal independence for Taiwan. All are opposed to the use of force to resolve the Taiwan question. Most have important economic relations with Taiwan and, in order to expand those relations, have been willing to exchange visits by ministerial or higher level officials, as well as to conclude air transport, shipping, and other agreements—even when Beijing has protested those actions. There is considerable admiration among the people of these countries, nearly all of which are democracies, for the success of the people of Taiwan in transforming their political system from authoritarianism to democracy. They sympathize with the desire of the people of Taiwan to expand their international space, but, like the people of the United States, they hesitate to go too far in collaborating with this endeavor for fear of damaging important relations with the PRC and increasing the risk that Beijing's leaders might feel compelled to use military force against Taiwan.[13]

Representative of the views of many of these countries was a statement by Senior Minister Lee Kwan Yew of Singapore in January 1996 advocating that Taiwan maintain a low profile internationally, while expanding its economic and cultural links with the world and simultaneously increasing its people-to-people ties with mainland China. "Gradually, over fifty to sixty years," Lee said "the wide differences that have developed since 1949 will narrow, especially the differences between Fujian province and Taiwan. For either side to preempt or pressure-cook the outcome is to risk unnecessary losses for both. On the other hand, slow, gradual but continual increases in economic, cultural and social ties will benefit both sides. . . . Gradualism is the best way forward."[14]

Given the common interests of all these countries in opposing conflict in the Taiwan Strait and encouraging cooperation between Taiwan and mainland China, the United States should be more active than in the past in consulting with them on ways of discouraging conflict and improving prospects for an eventual political settlement. In discussions between officials of these countries and the PRC, the point could be stressed that conflict in the Taiwan Strait would not be simply an internal matter for China, but would have a damaging effect on the entire region. Warnings from a number of countries against the use of force, combined with expressions of approbation for the progress being made in creating a linkage community across the strait, would strengthen the hand of moderates in the PRC who would not like to see the Taiwan issue weaken international support for China's drive toward modernization.

Like the United States, these countries are concerned about political trends in Taiwan and the risk that a DPP government, by totally rejecting any form of unification with mainland China, might reverse the trend toward cooperation and set the stage for combat. Consultations between the United States and concerned countries are needed, so that a common approach could dispel any illusions in Taiwan that a move toward de jure independence would receive international backing.

Consultations on minimizing the risk of conflict should include consideration of how to induce the PRC to allow the people of Taiwan to have greater scope for action in the international community, such as some form of participation in the IMF, as discussed later in this chapter. A cooperative effort over a considerable period of time probably would be necessary, as was the case years ago in persuading the PRC to accept Taiwan's membership in the ADB and APEC. Moreover, following the U.S. example of highlighting and publicizing Taiwan's activities in the intergovernmental organizations to which it already belongs would demonstrate these countries' approval of the cooperation between Beijing and Taipei in the international arena. Publicity abroad for these activities would be picked up by the Taiwan media, easing the Taiwan people's sense of international isolation.

Building a Constructive Relationship with the PRC

Aside from pursuing the policies discussed here, directly related to the Taiwan issue, the United States should continue to work toward a broad, constructive strategic partnership with the PRC, giving this effort the attention merited by China's growing importance in the world community. The Clinton administration made progress in this regard in 1997–1998 through the exchange of presidential and other official visits and the increased cooperation in various areas that has accompanied the institutionalization of these official exchanges.

Maintaining good relations with China is not easy. Wide differences in standard of living, systems of governance, and basic political philosophy lead to misperceptions and misunderstandings between the two countries. The American view of China is strongly influenced by the memory of Tiananmen and the fact that China is the largest remaining country governed by a Communist Party. The Chinese view of the United States is affected by the history of past humiliation and an ingrained suspicion (or, in many cases, conviction) that the fundamental U.S. goal is hegemony over East Asia.[15] The complexities and difficulties of carrying out an effective overall China policy cannot be dealt with here; most analysts concede that alternating periods of tension and relaxation are inevitable.[16]

The point being made here is that improving overall relations with the PRC makes the Taiwan issue easier to manage. The more that PRC leaders value the U.S. relationship as a contribution to China's modernization, the more reluctant they are likely to be to jeopardize it over the Taiwan issue. Of course, if they were convinced that force had to be used to prevent Taiwan from going independent, they would not be deterred by risk to the U.S. relationship. Short of that extreme, however, the U.S. factor would be a consideration in their policy toward Taiwan. If there were a debate within the PRC over Taiwan policy, for example, the perception that a hard-line policy toward Taiwan would halt a favorable trend in U.S.-PRC relations could enable the moderates to prevail.

Similarly, when U.S.-PRC overall relations deteriorate, the volume of recriminations against the United States over the Taiwan issue is likely to increase. Resentment over U.S. actions on other issues tends to stimulate the endemic fear that hegemonistic Americans are engaged in trying to detach Taiwan permanently from China.

Encouraging Beijing-Taipei Dialogue

U.S. officials and other Americans have urged Beijing and Taipei to open a dialogue, either through the resumption of the suspended SEF-ARATS channel or in some other way. Some Americans, pointing to the active U.S. role in promoting negotiations in the Middle East and Bosnia, have advocated a more active U.S. role in getting cross-strait negotiations started. The official U.S. position for the past twenty years, however, has been that the cross-strait differences should be resolved by the people on both sides of the strait. The only concern of the United States was that the resolution be peaceful.

The preponderance of views on the China mainland and in Taiwan accords with this U.S. position. The PRC has asserted, as a basic principle, that mainland China-Taiwan relations are a domestic matter in which foreigners should not interfere. On the Taiwan side, government officials and the media have expressed concern that the United States might exert pressure on Taiwan to accept PRC conditions for negotiation. Hence, they have placed considerable emphasis on the "six assurances" of July 1982, in which the United States assured the ROC that it would not play any mediating role between Taipei and Beijing and that it would not exert pressure on the ROC to enter into negotiations with the PRC.[17]

In April 1998 the formal SEF-ARATS meetings, suspended since June 1995, resumed with a visit to Beijing by SEF's deputy secretary-general. The two sides agreed that Koo Chen-fu would visit the PRC during 1998 to meet with his counterpart, Wang Daohan. As Beijing and Taipei move ahead with a dialogue, the best role for the United States will continue to be that of a friendly bystander, refraining from expressing views on the details of the negotiation. To do so would risk being drawn into the dispute, with each side trying to manipulate the outsider. Left to themselves, the two Chinese sides probably could tolerate a prolonged period of negotiation, whereas an American mediator, under pressure from an impatient Congress and public, would tend, unrealistically, to seek an early solution.

Avoiding Confrontation

The United States cannot avoid taking some actions that will be perceived by the PRC as fostering a separate Taiwan rather than as promoting unification. The foremost, in Beijing's eyes, is the assertion of firm opposition to the use of force against Taiwan and the supply of advanced arms to the island. Others include contacts between senior U.S. and ROC officials, which are deemed necessary by the governments in Washington and Taipei to promote economic and other relations between the people of Taiwan and the United States; permission for the president, vice president, or premier of the ROC to transit the United States in their efforts to enhance Taiwan's international status; and U.S. actions to help win membership or participation by Taiwan in intergovernmental organizations.

In taking these unavoidable actions, the United States should try to minimize the perception in Beijing that they are aimed at promoting the establishment of an independent state of Taiwan, mainly by keeping their efforts low key, while highlighting and expressing approval of growing cooperation between the people of Taiwan and mainland China. Strengthening Taiwan militarily and economically is not only a necessary U.S. response to political pressures in Taiwan and the United States, but it will increase support in Taiwan for the view that the ROC can confidently expand the mutually beneficial economic interaction across the strait and eventually work out with Beijing an agreement on political association.

Deterring Military Action

The United States has provided the primary deterrent to a military attack on Taiwan, first, by supplying the island with weapons to defend itself, and, second, by giving notice that it might, in some circumstances, intervene directly with U.S. forces. Ever since President Harry Truman ordered the 7th Fleet to prevent an attack on Taiwan in 1950, the United States has been involved in the defense of the island. After the abrogation of the security treaty in 1979, the Taiwan Relations Act provided that the United States would continue to supply defensive weapons, declared that the use of force against Taiwan would be of grave concern to the United States, and directed the government to maintain the capacity to resist any such use of force.

Taiwan's defense forces are designed to make an attack on the island very costly, and the possibility that U.S. forces might intervene adds a further deterrent. It would be unwise, however, to become too reliant on military deterrents. As mainland China becomes stronger, economically and militarily, it will become increasingly difficult to maintain anything approaching a military balance between the forces in Taiwan and those on the mainland. The only way to prevent Taiwan from becoming increasingly dependent on the willingness of the American people to intervene militarily is to reduce the need for military deterrence by the development of a growing cooperative relationship between Taiwan and mainland China and to keep open the prospect of some form of unification.

For a few years there is a window of opportunity during which Taiwan will not need new major weapons systems from the United States. The military in Taiwan will be fully occupied with incorporating the advanced weapons systems currently being delivered from the United States and France or produced domestically.[18] Moreover, the deficit in the national budget, the government's goal of a balanced budget by 2001, and the growing demands for domestic expenditures, driven by increasingly competitive politics, inhibit heavy new outlays for weapons. Plans must be made, of course, for continued modernization of Taiwan's armed forces in the future, but reducing the need for weapons by improved cross-strait relations should be the priority for the next few years.

The United States should from time to time reiterate its expectation, as it indicated when it signed the joint communiqués of 1979 and 1982, that the final resolution of the Taiwan question will be peaceful. It could draw attention to instances of cross-strait cooperation and negotiation as evidence of progress toward that goal. At the same time, it will have to maintain a military presence in the western Pacific that is capable of intervening should cross-strait relations deteriorate severely. For the time being, the United States should avoid providing new, high-profile weapons systems to Taiwan. However, a continuing flow of items will be needed to maintain and improve the defensive equipment of the ROC's armed forces, as provided by the Taiwan Relations Act. This ongoing activity should be kept as low-key as possible. The purpose of the United States should be to hold the military option in reserve, not to facilitate the gaining of de jure independence for Taiwan but to encourage the two sides to work toward an increasingly cooperative relationship. Thus, the PRC would not have a free hand to resolve the Taiwan question quickly by the use of force, nor could pro-independence advocates rely on the United States to protect Taiwan if they moved quickly to achieve de jure independence. Patience is needed on both sides, a willingness to live with a degree of uncertainty regarding the future. The United States cannot commit itself either to intervene or not to intervene militarily, but it can and should commit itself to support in every possible way growing cooperation between the people and governments on the two sides of the strait.

Seeking Taiwan's Participation in the IMF

The 1997–1998 financial crisis in East Asia demonstrated the disadvantage of Taiwan's being unable to contribute to the IMF's efforts to stabilize the economic situation. Since Taiwan is the fourteenth largest trading nation, a member of the ADB and APEC, and a prospective member of the WTO, with a strong economy and ample foreign exchange reserves, a strong case can be made for its participation in IMF activities. Moreover, Taiwan was criticized for the damaging effect on neighboring countries of its October 1997 decision to allow the Taiwan dollar to depreciate. If Taiwan had been a member or an associate of the IMF, it would have been in closer touch with the thinking of financial decision makers and high-level channels would have been available through which to urge Taiwan not to devalue.

Overcoming PRC opposition to IMF participation would require devising a special form of participation by Taiwan under the name "Chinese Taipei." International support would have to be mobilized among the most influential members of the IMF, and the ROC might offer a trade-off in the form of easing restrictions on the "three links" or on Taiwan investment on the mainland. Success in this effort, by demonstrating that the PRC could tolerate some expansion of Taiwan's international space, would make it easier to win support in Taiwan for closer economic cooperation with mainland China.

In discussing with the PRC the desirability of some form of IMF participation by Taiwan, U.S. officials and those of other friendly countries could stress the contribution that mainland China, Hong Kong, and Taiwan are making to the economic growth of the region, underlining how greater cooperation between them in the international arena would be beneficial to all three. The IMF would provide an additional important venue for such cooperation.

Carefully Handling Visits by ROC Officials

The PRC's abrasive reaction to Lee Teng-hui's Cornell visit forcefully demonstrated the determination of Beijing's leaders not to tolerate trips abroad by top ROC officials, especially to the United States, that would bolster a claim by Taiwan to be a separate, sovereign state. Following the military confrontation of March 1996, the U.S. government adopted a cautious attitude concerning such visits, not ruling them out but indicating that they would be rare, private, and considered on a case-by-case basis. Vice President Lien Chan has been granted transit visas to pass through American cities en route to other destinations on the condition that he not hold a press conference during his stopovers. The United States also issued a transit visa to Lee Teng-hui to pass through Honolulu en route to and from Central America in September 1997. The PRC protested the issuance of the visa, but, as the stopovers occurred with a minimum of publicity and did not include press conferences on U.S. soil, the U.S.-PRC overall relationship was not significantly affected.

Restricting visits by top officials of a friendly government is difficult for the United States. Yet past experience has shown that failure to heed Beijing's sensitivity to such visits can result in severe deterioration of U.S.-PRC relations and an increased risk of military action in the Taiwan Strait. This seems a high price to pay to modestly heighten Taiwan's international status and the domestic popularity of a Taiwan politician. Consequently, it would be wise to continue the present policy of carefully handling the occasional visits by Taiwan's top leaders.

Conclusion

In order to avoid being drawn into a costly, unwanted military conflict with the PRC over Taiwan, ways must be found for Americans to join forces with the moderate center in both the mainland and Taiwan. The great majority of people in both places would prefer the gradual expansion of peaceful interaction across the strait rather than an attempt to bridge the political gap by demanding early unification or independence. But extremists on both sides of the strait press urgently for their preferred solution. Extremists on the mainland want agreement on unification as soon as possible to check the trend toward Taiwan independence represented by the growing political influence of the DPP. Extremists in Taiwan want to establish a "Republic of Taiwan" (with U.S. support and international recognition) before the PRC becomes too strong.

Persuading Americans that the people of Taiwan deserve recognition as an independent state is not difficult. Taiwan has functioned as a de facto independent state for many years and meets the qualifications prescribed by international law for independent statehood. Americans are linked to the people of Taiwan by long-standing and growing ties—economic, institutional, family, and personal. Taiwan's outstanding achievement of rapid economic growth and its transformation from an authoritarian to a democratic society have won widespread admiration in the United States. To stand by and allow Taiwan to be forcibly integrated into the PRC would be very difficult for Americans, who have bound themselves by the Taiwan Relations Act to regard any such attempt with grave concern and to supply the people of Taiwan with defensive arms.

For Americans, it is far easier to sympathize with the people of Taiwan than to understand how a much larger number of Chinese in mainland China view "the Taiwan problem." These Chinese perceive that China has been kept divided by U.S. intervention in 1950 to prevent the "liberation" of Taiwan. They see the continuing U.S. support of Taiwan as making possible the continued separate existence of the island and as blocking the final unification of all Chinese territory. For many of them, unification is an essential step in China's drive to achieve the status of a major power in the twenty-first century.

It is easier for Americans to side unthinkingly with friendly Taiwan than to recognize the need to develop a constructive relationship with Beijing that will contribute to a peaceful resolution of the Taiwan issue. The government of the PRC is rightfully criticized for its one-party system, its lack of a free press, and its repression of dissidents, including the Christian minority that rejects state control. The United States has serious differences with the PRC over the proliferation of weapons of mass destruction, the accession of China to the World Trade Organization, and the large and growing trade surplus with the United States.

All these differences, plus the potential threat of a militarily powerful China, are exaggerated by extremists of the Right and the Left in the United States. Sometimes the differences are exploited for domestic political advantage. It is relatively easy to gain support for sense of the Congress resolutions condemning the PRC or urging U.S. sanctions against it, thus creating a division between Congress and the administration.

While acknowledging the differences between Washington and Beijing, it is also important for Americans to recognize that China is changing. Economic development over the past twenty years has improved the standard of living of the great majority of Chinese and they have much greater freedom of speech and action than they had under the totalitarian rule of the past. Calls for political reform are increasingly heard. American willingness to take a balanced view of changing China will make it easier for the U.S. government to pursue a China policy that minimizes the risk of military conflict over Taiwan.

Moreover, a strong case can be made—as the Clinton administration has recently sought to do—for finding ways to cooperate with an increasingly powerful China in order to draw it into a constructive relationship with the world community. The United States not only has serious differences with China, but it also has a variety of common interests, from assuring a stable, nonnuclear Korean peninsula to protecting the environment and suppressing the trade in illegal drugs.

It is essential for Americans to recognize the power of Chinese nationalism on the China mainland. To confront it head-on provides ammunition to the extremists in the PRC, who attack the United States for trying to contain China. Americans must soberly consider how much they would be willing to pay to ensure the full independence for Taiwan demanded by some politicians there, if the cost might mean war with the PRC. Americans might better appreciate the strength of the demand for unification in the PRC by recalling the U.S. civil war, in which Union forces fought for four bloody years to prevent the Confederate States of America from seceding from the Union and forming a separate nation.

It is often difficult to build support for compromise with the PRC without being accused of "kowtowing to the tyrants in Beijing." Yet the best way to support friends in Taiwan is to prevent military conflict in the strait, which would be devastating to them. The United States must be willing to urge agreement on a middle ground, which will not be totally satisfactory to those on either side of the strait.

For Beijing and Taipei to reach a compromise that both can live with will not be easy and will require prolonged negotiations. But if both governments encourage the expansion of people-to-people interaction across the strait, do not insist on early agreement, and keep the door open for some form of unification, a status quo that is satisfactory to most people on both sides of the strait can be maintained and pressures by the extremists can be contained.

The United States can contribute significantly to an eventual peaceful resolution of the Taiwan issue by holding firmly to established policy—opposing any resort to force in the Taiwan Strait, continuing to supply defensive arms to Taiwan, refusing to support Taiwan independence or Taiwan participation in the United Nations, and encouraging a cross-strait dialogue while insisting that the eventual solution of the Taiwan problem must be worked out by those on the two sides of the strait, without U.S. mediation or invervention. The United States should resist any effort by Beijing or Taipei to persuade it to pressure the other side. It should also publicize and applaud the expansion of mutually beneficial cross-strait, people-to-people interaction and the gradual creation of a linkage community within which mistrust is diminished and the prospect for eventual political agreement is enhanced.

Given the wide differences between Beijing and Taipei on the future of Taiwan, no early resolution of the problem is likely. The two governments and concerned individuals on both sides of the strait will criticize U.S. policy and try to bend it in directions that they favor. Many Americans will be uncomfortable with a policy that does not take a clearcut stand in support of one side or the other and leaves the Taiwan problem unresolved for a long time to come. Yet in order to minimize the risk of conflict in the Taiwan Strait, the United States must take account of views on both sides of the strait and pursue a policy that helps to preserve a status quo that the great majority of people on both sides of the strait can live with.

Notes

1. President Bill Clinton's address to the Asia Society and the U.S.-China Educational Foundation, October 24, 1997.

2. For the text of the Shanghai communiqué, see Stephen P. Gibert and William M. Carpenter, *America and Island China: A Documentary History* (Lanham, MD: University Press of America, 1989), pp. 111–114.

3. *Ibid.,* pp. 296–297, 312–314.

4. Lee Teng-hui, *Creating the Future: Towards a New Era for the Chinese People* (Taipei: Government Information Office, September, 1993), pp. 7–9.

5. Ralph N. Clough, *Reaching Across the Taiwan Strait* (Boulder, CO: Westview Press, 1993), p. 132.

6. Mainland Affairs Council, Taipei, *Relations Across the Taiwan Strait* (July 1994) p. 33.

7. See Secretary of State Warren Christopher's speech at Fudan University, Shanghai, November 21, 1996; speech by Samuel R. Berger, Assistant to the President for National Security Affairs, to the Council on Foreign Relations, New York, June 6, 1997 and address by President Bill Clinton, Oct. 24, 1997.

8. *Xinhua*, in English (October 30, 1997 [*FBIS-CHI-97-303*]; *New York Times* (October 30, 1997): 18.

9. *China Post* (May 20, 1996). For the U.S. statement that it would not support Taiwan independence, see White House press release of October 29, 1997 (p. 5), containing a background press briefing by "a senior administration official" reporting on President Clinton's discussion with President Jiang. See also Department of State Daily Press Briefing Index for October 31, 1997 (p. 11), quoting press briefer James P. Rubin.

10. *China Times.* <www.Chinatimes.com> (March 18,1998).

11. Clinton and Jiang's joint press conference, *New York Times* (October 30, 1997): 18.

12. *Washington Times* (April 7, 1998).

13. See, for example, Jusuf Wanandi, *Southeast Asia–Chinese Relations* (Taipei: Chinese Council for Advanced Policy Studies, CAPS Papers No. 13, Richard H. Yang, ed., Dec. 1996) p. 19.

14. *The Straits Times* (January 2, 1996): 2.

15. David Shambaugh, *Beautiful Imperialist: China Perceives America, 1972–1990* (Princeton: Princeton University Press, 1992), pp. 296–303.

16. Samuel S. Kim, "Taiwan and the International System: The Challenge of Legitimation," in Robert Sutter and William Johnson, eds., *Taiwan in World Affairs* (Boulder, CO: Westview Press, 1994), pp. 145–184. Also Harry Harding, *A Fragile Relationship: The United States and China Since 1972* (Washington, D.C.: Brookings Institution, 1992), Ezra Vogel, ed., *Living with China: U.S.-China Relations in the Twenty-first Century* (American Assembly, New York: W. W. Norton, 1997), Morton Abramowitz, *China: Can We Have a Policy?* (Carnegie Endowment for International Peace, Washington, D.C.: Brookings Institution Press, 1997).

17. *ROC Statement on August 17 Communiqué*, Gibert and Carpenter, *America and Island China*, pp. 325–326.

18. For a comparison of PRC and Taiwan arms modernization programs, see Richard A. Bitzinger, "Military Spending and Foreign Military Acquisitions by the PRC and Taiwan," and Bates Gill, "Chinese Military Hardware and Technology Acquisitions of Concern to Taiwan," in James R. Lilley and Chuck Downs, eds., *Crisis in the Taiwan Strait* (Washington, D.C.: National Defense University Press, 1997).

Bibliography

Books and Documents

Abramowitz, Morton. *China: Can We Have a Policy?* Carnegie Endowment for International Peace, Washington, D.C.: Brookings Institution Press, 1997.

Barnett, A. Doak, and others. *Developing a Peaceful, Stable and Cooperative Relationship with China*. New York: National Committee on American Foreign Policy, July 1996.

Berger, Samuel. *Building a New Consensus on China*. Remarks before Council on Foreign Relations, June 6, 1997.

Chan, Gerald. *China and International Organizations: Participation in Non-Governmental Organizations Since 1971*. Hong Kong: Oxford University Press, 1989.

Chang Jaw-Ling, Joanne, ed. *ROC-US Relations, 1979–1989*. Taipei: Academia Sinica, 1991.

Chang, Parris, and Martin Lasater, eds. *If the PRC Crosses the Yalu: The International Response*. Lanham, MD: University Press of America, 1993.

Cheng Lang-ping. *Yi Jiu Jiu Wu, Jun Ba Yue (The Warning of Taiwan Strait War)*. Taipei: Shang Chou Wen Hua Shih Yeh, 1994.

Christopher, Warren. *Building a New Era of Cooperation for a New Century*. Speech at Fudan University. Shanghai, Nov. 22, 1996.

Clinton, Bill. *Remarks by the President in Address on China and the National Interest before Asia Society and U.S.-China Educational Foundation*. Oct. 24, 1997.

Clough, Ralph N. *Reaching Across the Taiwan Strait: People-to-People Diplomacy*. Boulder, CO: Westview Press, 1993.

Council for Economic Planning and Development. *Taiwan Statistical Data Book, 1996*. Taipei.

Democratic Progressive Party Charter and Program. Taipei, Aug. 1, 1995.

Finkelstein, David M. *Washington's Taiwan Dilemma: From Abandonment to Salvation*. Fairfax, VA: George Mason University Press, 1993.

Garver, John W. *Face-Off: China, the United States and Taiwan's Democratization*. Seattle: The University of Washington Press, 1997.

Government Information Office. *The Republic of China Yearbook, 1993*. Taipei.

Harding, Harry. *A Fragile Relationship: The United States and China Since 1972*. Washington, D.C.: Brookings Institution, 1992.

Holmes, Kim R., and Thomas G. Moore, eds. *Restoring American Leadership.* Washington, D.C.: Heritage Foundation, 1996.

Hood, Steven J. *The KMT and the Democratization of Taiwan.* Boulder, CO: Westview Press, 1997.

Lardy, Nicholas. *China in the World Economy.* Washington, D.C.: Institute for International Economics, 1994.

Lasater, Martin. *U.S. Interests in the New Taiwan.* Boulder, CO: Westview Press, 1993.

Lilley, James R., and Chuck Downs, eds. *Crisis in the Taiwan Strait.*Washington, D.C.: National Defense University Press, 1997.

Mainland Affairs Council. *Beyond the Historical Gap: Retrospect and Prospect of Ten Years' Cross-Strait Exchanges.* Taipei, August 1, 1997.

Mainland Affairs Council. *Cross-Strait Exchanges: The ROC Government's Liberalization Measures and Mainland China's Blocking Attempts.* Taipei, Sept. 1997.

Mainland Affairs Council. *Public Opinion on Cross-Strait Relations in the Republic of China.* Taipei, April 1, 1997.

Mainland Affairs Council. *The Republic of China's Policy Toward Hong Kong and Macao.* Taipei, May 1996.

Miles, James. *The Legacy of Tiananmen: China in Disarray.* Ann Arbor: University of Michigan, 1996.

Munro, Ross, and Richard Bernstein. *The Coming Conflict with China.* New York: Alfred A. Knopf, 1997.

National Development Conference Secretariat. *National Development Conference Resolutions.* Taipei, Jan. 1997.

Ross, Robert, and Andrew J. Nathan. *The Great Wall and the Empty Fortress.* New York: Norton, 1997

Shambaugh, David. *Beautiful Imperialist: China Perceives America, 1972–1990.* Princeton: Princeton University Press, 1992.

State Council, Taiwan Affairs Office and Information Office. *The Taiwan Question and the Reunification of China.* Beijing, August, 1993.

Sutter, Robert, and William Johnson, eds. *Taiwan in World Affairs.* Boulder, CO: Westview Press, 1994.

Vogel, Ezra, ed. *Living with China: US-China Relations in the Twenty-First Century.* American Assembly, New York: W. W. Norton, 1997.

Wanandi, Jusuf. *Southeast Asia–China Relations.* Taipei: CAPS Papers No. 13, Chinese Council of Advanced Policy Studies, December 1996.

Wei, Yung. *From "Multi-System Nations" to "Linkage Communities."* Occasional Papers/Reprint Series in Contemporary Asian Studies, no. 1, 1998 (Baltimore, MD: School of Law, University of Maryland).

Newspapers and Periodicals

Beijing Review
Central People's Radio
Cheng Ts'e Yueh Kan (Policy Monthly)

Chiao Liu
China Post
Chung Kuo Shih Pao (China Times)
Chung Yang Jih Pao (Central Daily News)
Chung Yang She (Central News Agency)
Economic Daily News
Far Eastern Economic Review
Free China Journal
Free China Review
Fujian Ribao
Hsin Hsin Wen
International Journal
Issues and Studies
Journal of Contemporary China
Liaowang
Lien Ho Pao (United Daily News)
MAC News Briefing
New York Times
Renmin Ribao (People's Daily)
Shih Chieh Jih Pao (World Journal)
Sing Tao Jih Pao
The Straits Times
Ta Kung Pao
Tzuli Choupao (Independence Post Weekly)
Washington Post
Wen Hui Pao (Wen Wei Po)
Xinhua
Zhongguo Tongxun She

Annex 1:
Jiang Zemin's Eight Points

(From his speech of January 30, 1995, entitled "Continue to Promote the Reunification of the Motherland")

1. Adherence to the principle of one China is the basis and premise for peaceful reunification. China's sovereignty and territory must never be allowed to suffer [a] split. We must firmly oppose any words or actions aimed at creating an "independent Taiwan" and the propositions "split the country and rule under separate regimes," "two Chinas over a certain period of time," etc., which are in contravention of the principle of one China.

2. We do not challenge the development of nongovernmental economic and cultural ties by Taiwan with other countries. Under the principle of one China and in accordance with the charters of the relevant international organizations, Taiwan has become a member of the Asian Development Bank, the Asia-Pacific Economic Cooperation forum, and other international economic organizations in the name of "Chinese Taipei." However, we oppose Taiwan's activities in "expanding its living space internationally," which are aimed at creating "two Chinas" or "one China, one Taiwan." All patriotic compatriots in Taiwan and other people of insight understand that instead of solving the problems, such activities can only help the forces working for the "independence of Taiwan" undermine the process of peaceful reunification more unscrupulously. Only after the peaceful reunification is accomplished can the Taiwan compatriots and other Chinese people of all ethnic groups truly and fully share the dignity and honor attained by our great motherland internationally.

3. It has been our consistent stand to hold negotiations with the Taiwan authorities on the peaceful reunification of the motherland. Repre-

sentatives from the various political parties and mass organizations on both sides of the Taiwan Straits can be invited to participate in such talks. I said in my report at the Fourteenth National Congress of the Communist Party of China held in October 1992, "On the premise that there is only one China, we are prepared to talk with the Taiwan authorities about any matter, including the form that official negotiations should take, a form that would be acceptable to both sides." By "on the premise that there is only one China, we are prepared to talk with the Taiwan authorities about any matter," we mean naturally that all matters of concern to the Taiwan authorities are included. We have proposed time and again that negotiations should be held on officially ending the state of hostility between the two sides and accomplishing peaceful reunification step by step. Here again I solemnly propose that such negotiations be held. I suggest that, as the first step, negotiations should be held and an agreement reached on officially ending the state of hostility between the two sides in accordance with the principle that there is only one China. On this basis, the two sides should undertake jointly to safeguard China's sovereignty and territorial integrity and map out plans for the future development of their relations. As regards the name, place, and form of these political talks, a solution acceptable to both sides can certainly be found so long as consultations on an equal footing can be held at an early date.

4. We should strive for the peaceful reunification of the motherland since Chinese should not fight fellow Chinese. Our not undertaking to give up the use of force is not directed against our compatriots in Taiwan but against the schemes of foreign forces to interfere with China's reunification and to bring about the "independence of Taiwan." We are fully confident that our compatriots in Taiwan, Hong Kong, and Macao and those residing overseas would understand our principled position.

5. In [the] face of the development of the world economy in the twenty-first century, great efforts should be made to expand the economic exchanges and cooperation between the two sides of the Taiwan Straits so as to achieve prosperity on both sides to the benefit of the entire Chinese nation. We hold that political differences should not affect or interfere with the economic cooperation between the two sides. We shall continue to implement over a long period of time the policy of encouraging industrialists and businesspeople from Taiwan to invest in the mainland and enforce the Law of the People's Republic of China for Protecting the Investment of the Compatriots of Taiwan. Whatever the circumstances may be, we shall safeguard the legitimate rights and interests of industrialists and businesspeople from Taiwan. We should continue to expand contacts and exchanges between our compatriots on both sides so as to increase mutual understanding and

trust. Since the direct links for postal, air, and shipping services and trade between the two sides are the objective requirements for their economic development and contacts in various fields, and since they are in the interests of the people on both sides, it is absolutely necessary to adopt practical measures to speed up the establishment of such direct links. Efforts should be made to promote negotiations on certain specific issues between the two sides. We are in favor of conducting this kind of negotiations on the basis of reciprocity and mutual benefit and signing non-governmental agreements on the protection of the rights and interests of industrialists and businesspeople from Taiwan.

6. The splendid culture of five thousand years created by the sons and daughters of all ethnic groups of China has become ties keeping the entire Chinese people close at heart and constitutes an important basis for the peaceful reunification of the motherland. People on both sides of the Taiwan Strait should inherit and carry forward the fine traditions of the Chinese culture.

7. The twenty-one million compatriots in Taiwan, whether born there or in other provinces, are all Chinese and our own flesh and blood. We should fully respect their lifestyle and their wish to be the masters of our country and protect all their legitimate rights and interests. The relevant departments of our party and the government including the agencies stationed abroad should strengthen close ties with compatriots from Taiwan, listen to their views and demands, be concerned with and take into account their interests and make every effort to help them solve their problems. We hope that Taiwan Island enjoys social stability, economic growth and affluence. We also hope that all political parties in Taiwan will adopt a sensible, forward-looking, and constructive attitude and promote the expansion of relations between the two sides. All parties and personages of all circles in Taiwan are welcome to exchange views with us on relations between the two sides and on peaceful reunification and are also welcome to pay a visit and tour places. All personages from various circles who have contributed to the reunification of China will go down in history for their deeds.

8. Leaders of the Taiwan authorities are welcome to pay visits in appropriate capacities. We are also ready to accept invitations from the Taiwan side to visit Taiwan. We can discuss state affairs or exchange ideas on certain questions first. Even a simple visit to the other side will be useful. The affairs of the Chinese people should be handled by ourselves, something that does not take an international occasion to accomplish. Separated across the Straits, our people eagerly look forward to meeting each other.

Annex 2:
Lee Teng-hui's Six Points

(From his speech to the National Unification Council, April 8, 1995)

1. Seek China's unification on the reality of separate rules across the strait.

Since 1949, Taiwan and the mainland have been governed by two political entities which were not subordinated to one another, and this created the situation of the two shores of the strait being split and separately governed. This is why we now have the national unification issue. Therefore, to solve the unification problem, we must be pragmatic and respect history and should seek a feasible way for national unification based on the fact that the two shores are separately governed. Only by objectively treating this reality can the two shores gain more common understanding on the meaning of "one China" as soon as possible.

2. Step up cross-strait exchange on the basis of the Chinese culture.

The broad and profound Chinese culture is the common pride and spiritual base of all Chinese people. We have always made it our job to maintain and develop our traditional culture and also propose that the culture be used as the basis for cross-strait exchange in order to elevate the national sentiment of common existence and common prosperity and to foster and treasure the brotherly sentiment. In the vast cultural sphere, the two shores should increase the breadth and depth of exchanges, and further increase exchange and cooperation in the information, academic, science and technology, sports and other fields.

3. Increase cross-strait economic and trade exchanges and develop mutually beneficiary and supplementary relations.

Faced with the global trend of going all out to develop the economy, Chinese should supplement and benefit each other and share experiences with each other. Taiwan should make mainland China its hinterland in developing its economy, whereas mainland China should draw lessons from Taiwan in developing its economy. We are willing to provide technology and experiences to assist mainland China in improving its agriculture, so as to bring benefit to the broad masses of peasants. In the meantime, we will continue to help mainland China promote economic prosperity on the basis of existing investment and trade. As the issues concerning cross-strait business and shipping exchanges are quite complicated, departments concerned must approach such issues in many aspects, make early planning, and when the time and conditions are ripe, personnel on the two sides may communicate with each other in specified places, so as to thoroughly understand the problems and exchange views.

4. Two sides join international organizations on equal footing and leaders of the two sides will naturally meet each other on such occasions.

I have repeated many times that natural meetings of leaders from the two sides on international occasions will ease political confrontation between the two sides and foster an atmosphere of harmonious contacts and meetings. Now the two sides have joined several important international economic and sports organizations. If leaders from both sides meet each other naturally while attending meetings of such organizations, it will surely help eliminate hostility between the two sides, build up mutual trust, and lay a foundation for future consultation and cooperation. We believe that the more international organizations the two sides join on an equal footing, the more it will be conducive to developing bilateral relations and to promoting the process of peaceful reunification. This will also show the world that the Chinese people on the two sides, despite political differences, can still join hands to make contributions to the international community and create a new age for the Chinese nation to stand proud in the world.

5. Two sides should persist in using peaceful means to resolve disputes.

The descendants of Emperors Yan and Huang should first show sincerity to each other and no longer engage in fratricide. We do not want the Chinese people to go down the path of civil war once again and hope that hostility will be turned into friendship. In 1991 the ROC announced the end of the Period of Mobilization for the Suppression of the Communist Rebellion, acknowledged that the two sides were separated, and announced that it would no longer use force against the mainland. It is regrettable that over the last four years the Chinese Communist authorities have not announced [their] renunciation of the use of force against Taiwan, Penghu, and Kinmen and Matsu, causing the continuation of the situation of the hostile confrontation up to this day. We hold that the mainland authorities should show their goodwill by renouncing the use of force against Taiwan, Penghu, and Kinmen and Matsu, and that they should refrain from any military actions that could cause suspicions, thereby laying the foundation for ending the situation of hostile confrontation through formal cross-strait talks. I must emphasize that using the so-called "Taiwan independence forces" or "foreign interference" as a pretext for refusing to make the commitment to not use force against Taiwan is disregarding and distorting the founding spirit and policy of the ROC, which will only deepen suspicions between the two sides and hinder mutual trust. The degree of maturity for ending the situation of hostile confrontation through formal cross-strait talks requires sincere fostering by both sides. At present, we will have our relevant government departments carry out research and formulate plans concerning the termination of hostile confrontation. When the CCP officially announces its renunciation of the use of force against Taiwan, Penghu, and Kinmen and Matsu, a preliminary consultation on how to end the state of hostile confrontation between the two sides will be held at a most appropriate time and opportunity.

6. The two sides should jointly maintain the prosperity of and promote democracy in Hong Kong and Macao.

Hong Kong and Macao have always been Chinese territory. The people of Hong Kong and Macao are our brothers. We are deeply concerned about the situation in Hong Kong after 1997 and in Macao after 1999. The ROC government reiterates once again that it will continue to maintain normal ties with Hong Kong and Macao, further participate in their affairs, and actively render service to compatriots in Hong Kong and Macao. Maintaining economic prosperity and a free and democratic lifestyle is the desire of the people of Hong Kong and Macao, which is the concern not only of the Chinese nationals residing abroad but also of other countries in the world, and which is also the unavoidable responsibility of people on both sides of the strait. We hope that the mainland authorities will actively respond to the demands of the people in Hong Kong and Macao and pool the strength on both sides of the strait to jointly develop plans with the people of Hong Kong and Macao for their prosperity and stability.

Annex 3:
Excerpts from Lee Teng-hui's Inaugural Address May 20, 1996

All the major cultures originated in a very restricted area. The five-thousand-year Chinese culture also rose from a small region called Chung Yuan. Uniquely situated at the confluence of mainland and maritime cultures, Taiwan has been able in recent decades to preserve traditional culture on the one hand and to come into wide contact with Western democracy and science and modern business culture on the other. Equipped with a much higher level of education and development than in other parts of China, Taiwan is set to gradually exercise its leadership role in cultural development and take upon itself the responsibility for nurturing a new Chinese culture. . . .

Today the existence and development of the Republic of China on Taiwan has won international recognition and respect. In the new international order of today, such basic tenets as democracy, human rights, peace, and renunciation of force are universally adhered to; they are in full accord with the ideals upon which our country was founded. We will continue to promote pragmatic diplomacy in compliance with the principles of goodwill and reciprocity. By doing so we will secure for our 21.3 million people enough room for existence and development as well as the respect and treatment they deserve in the international arena. . . .

The Republic of China has always been a sovereign state. Disputes across the straits center around system and lifestyle; they have nothing to do with ethnic or cultural identity. Here in this country it is totally unnecessary or impossible to adopt the so-called course of "Taiwan independence." For over forty years, the two sides of the straits have been two separate jurisdictions due to various historical factors, but it is also true that both sides pursue eventual national unification. Only when both sides face up to the facts and engage in dialogue with profound sincerity and patience will they be able to find the solution to the unification question and work for the common welfare of the Chinese people.

Today, I will seriously call upon the two sides of the straits to deal straightforwardly with the momentous question of how to terminate the state of hostility between them, which will then make a crucial contribution to the historic tasks of unification. In the future, at the call of my country and with the support of its people, I would like to embark upon a journey of peace to mainland China taking with me the consensus and will of the 21.3 million people. I am also ready to meet with the top leadership of the Chinese Communists for a direct exchange of views in order to open up a new era of communication and cooperation between the two sides and ensure peace, stability and prosperity in the Asia-Pacific region. . . .

We believe that whatever is achieved by the Chinese in Taiwan can also be achieved by the Chinese in mainland China. We are willing to provide our developmental experience as an aid in mapping the direction of development in mainland China. The fruits of our hard work can be used to assist in enhancing the welfare of millions of our compatriots on the mainland. The Chinese on the two sides can thus join forces for the benefit of the prosperity and development of the Chinese nation as a whole.

Index

United Nations, 12; DPP and, 33; Educational, Scientific, and Cultural Organization (UNESCO), 77; PRC and, 17, 24, 72–73, 75–76; ROC and, 23, 32, 39, 70, 72, 81
United States: assumptions underlying policy, 114; in deterrence of China-Taiwan conflict, 124–26; economic interests of, 19–21; goal of, 114–15; international support for, 120–22; military actions, x, 6, 11–12; policy benefits to China and Taiwan, 119–20; policy on visits by ROC officials, 127; popular view of China, 8, 18–19, 21, 122, 128; position on independence of Taiwan, 24, 117, 128; position on Lee's visit to Cornell, 1–2, 88; position on use of force, ix, x–xi, 6, 12–13, 87, 124; strategic interests of, 17–19; strategy of, 115; values of, 21–22
United States-PRC relations: diplomatic, 18; economic, 19–20; military exercises and, 7–8; policies regarding, 113–31; PRC view of, 13, 122; recommendations for, 122–23
United States-Taiwan relations, 12–13; arms sales, 18, 39, 89, 124; economic, 20–21, 25; history of, 17–19, 23; recommendations for, 113–31

Vacation diplomacy, 1, 75. *See also* Pragmatic diplomacy
Vietnam, 12, 18
Vietnam War, 17–18, 21

Wang Daohan, chairman of ARATS, 34–36, 98, 124
Wang Guangdong, president of KYMCO, 54
Wang Jun, vice president of China Golf Association, 61
Wang Yung-ching, chairman of Formosa Plastics Group, 42, 57, 118
Washington Post, 2, 100, 110n33
Weapons proliferation, 19
Wei Chuan, 53
Wei Yung, KMT legislator, 77
Wei Yung, political scientist, 108
Wen Wei Po, 3, 35, 98
World Bank, 15, 81
World Health Organization, 77
World Trade Organization, 76, 81, 118, 120
World War II, 13
Wu Jin, ROC education minister, 60–61
Wu Po-hsiung, KMT secretary general, 83
Wu Shaozu, PRC Olympic Committee president, 61
Wu Yi, PRC bureaucrat, 55

Xie Hong, editor, 104
Xing Yun, Buddhist master, 59
Xinhua, 4

Yu Chi-chung, publisher, 99

Zhang Zongxu, mayor of Xiamen, 96
Zhou Enlai, leader of PRC, 12
Zhu Rongji, mayor of Shanghai, 59, 107

About the Author

Ralph N. Clough is a professorial lecturer and coordinator of the SAIS China Forum at the Nitze School of Advanced International Studies, the Johns Hopkins University, Washington, D.C. He is a retired Foreign Service Officer who was director for Chinese Affairs in the Department of State and served for thirteen years in various posts in mainland China, Hong Kong and Taiwan. He is the author of *Island China* and *Reaching Across the Taiwan Strait*.

5633 03 |

ook must be returned to the Library on the last date stamped below.

006